Love and flowers!
Olivier

Living Art
Style Your Home with Flowers

Olivier Giugni

with Sylvie Bigar

Photographs by Phillip Ennis

ATRIA BOOKS

New York   London   Toronto   Sydney

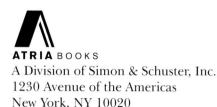
ATRIA BOOKS

A Division of Simon & Schuster, Inc.
1230 Avenue of the Americas
New York, NY 10020

Copyright © 2010 by L'Olivier Inc.

First Atria Books hardcover edition November 2010

ATRIA BOOKS and colophon are trademarks of Simon & Schuster, Inc.

For information about special discounts for bulk purchases, please contact Simon & Schuster Special Sales at 1-866-506-1949 or business@simonandschuster.com.

The Simon & Schuster Speakers Bureau can bring authors to your live event. For more information or to book an event contact the Simon & Schuster Speakers Bureau at 1-866-248-3049 or visit our website at www.simonspeakers.com.

Designed by Julian Peploe Studio
Olivier Giugni was responsible for the styling and *mise-en-scène* of the photography.
Micky Palmer Boulud was the project manager.

Manufactured in China

10   9   8   7   6   5   4   3   2   1

Library of Congress Cataloging-in-Publication Data
Giugni, Olivier.
    Living art : style your home with flowers / Olivier Giugni with Sylvie Bigar ; photographs by Phillip Ennis.
            p. cm.
Includes index.
1. Floral decorations. I. Bigar, Sylvie. II. Title.
SB449.G54 2010
745.92--dc22
                                    2010026227

ISBN 978-1-4391-0920-5
ISBN 978-1-4391-8417-2 (ebook)

To my dear friend Renée Clément, whose elegance, kindness, and sense of humor still shine in my heart.

Contents

At home nothing is impossible with
flowers, Freedom and Power!
Nature is all yours - Volume and
Textures are the major challenges

You must be audacious and
tame the extraordinary perfection
of vegetals - and that is
exactly what the book of Olivia's
has given to me - Dreams!

Amitiés

Catherine Deneuve

Preface

Les fleurs c'est la vie! (Flowers mean life!)
Looking down sixteen floors to the seemingly infinite green expanse of Central Park that stretches beyond my Harlem apartment to the height of Manhattan's sunny skyline, I reflect on my journey, laced with formidable opportunities and life-changing encounters.

Flowers make me happy. With cheer and joy, these colorful beings carry me through each day. Flowers hold the power to touch our hearts and convey their distinctive messages. Watching their miraculous cycle, from tight bud to full bloom, I am grateful for nature's ever-renewing miracle. I seek beauty everywhere I go. Today more than ever, as my life takes on a hectic pace, I derive happiness and peace from plants, both outdoors and at home, and I wake each morning more determined than ever to share this passion with others. With this book, I invite you to share in the love of flowers that infuses my artistic vision. I hope these pages will inspire you to pick up your own tools and surround yourself with nature and beauty.

As a young child, long before I knew I would spend my life in the company of flowers, I often found myself on my grandmother Lucie's terrace in Brignoles, a small medieval village between Aix-en-Provence and St. Tropez in the South of France. On her large deck, my first playground, she grew a variety of shiny succulents, ruby red geraniums, aromatic rosemary, thyme, lavender, ferns, pink laurel, and even a venerable fig tree. She enrolled me as her assistant gardener. I was in charge of watering, cleaning, and soon cutting the various plants. She would make homemade lemonade to reward me for my hard labor before we would sit down to plot our next gardening move. She was determined to have the most beautiful terrace in the village. My grandfather credits our gnarly olive trees, his proudest possessions, for my name, Olivier. On weekends, my mother, Nati, would take me to open-air flea markets and antique shows. She would patiently describe furnishings and objects, their various styles and *époques*. She also loved artifacts made from precious woods: walnut, ebony, and cherry. This was my first schooling in objets d'art.

I have always loved nature. Plants and animals. My uncle René and I went hunting with his frisky pointer, Portos, but I never allowed him to kill anything. He would say, "I'm taking the gun just in case." These hunts turned into long walks in the countryside. We fished in the local rivers but always let the fish go free. As trophies we would bring back oddly shaped pieces of wood, shiny stones, and wildflowers.

Picture the Var *vert,* where I was born. The green *garrigue* of southern Provence—where spring often brings lush shrubs and perennials, summer leads to steamy hot conditions, fall parades its mushrooms and grape harvest, and winter claims fame in the form of juicy, ripe olives. The various scents of this particular landscape are embedded in my soul. (I would later recapture them in the aromatic candle I created.) The seasons were marked by family celebrations. At Christmas and Easter, lavish tables were filled with flowers, fruit, and traditional dishes. On my father's side, my Italian grandmother made the best gnocchi; my mother's mother from Spain brought paella and tortillas. Our small vineyards produced the lovely stony rosé of the Bandol region, and meals always ended in joyous songs. My brother, Christophe, my sister, Béatrice, and I would take turns imitating the latest French pop stars, encouraged by laughs and applause.

As a dedicated choirboy, I was in the front row where I could observe the villagers in their Sunday best and always admired the very different but oh-so-fashionable outfits of my aunts, Yvonne and Cari. They taught me that high black patent leather boots were in and Nepalese purple scarves were out. Color and style already mattered for me.

Summers were spent at the beach in Hyères, where we picked shells and explored the rocks for shrimp, crabs, and sea urchins. I discovered the unusual beauty of seaweed and, to this day, often mix it into my arrangements. At night we went to the movies, and I soon developed my first and far from last crush: Brigitte Bardot, the sumptuous St. Tropez–based superstar.

It was always assumed that I would take over the family plumbing business, but I was not too keen on school, or skilled with a wrench for that matter. On my first workday, I spent all my time in the client's garden. My father called my mother and said he was sending me home. I wasn't destined to be a plumber after all.

I moved to St. Tropez during the high season and met numerous professionals whose opinions about my future all seemed to converge. I needed to go north, to Paris.

Struck by the beauty of the City of Light and thrilled to be a part of it, I quickly made friends. I would walk around the Place de la Concorde and take in the monuments, the trees, the impeccable flower beds on the Champs-Élysées. Keeping the treasured memory of my grandmother's magical terrace as a beacon, I began an apprenticeship in a Parisian neighborhood flower shop catering to the traditional customers of the Sixteenth Arrondissement.

I worked hard, learning all I could about flowers and plants—how to care for them, refining my cutting technique, and getting familiar with the business. I soon felt confident about my basic knowledge and techniques and started experimenting with unusual designs to the horror of my very conservative boss. He would say, "The métier of a florist is to send bouquets for important events or to say thank you after an evening or an invitation. Bouquets are made of cut flowers and that's it." Clients would then unwrap them and, with more or usually less skill, plunk them randomly into their own vases. As much as I enjoyed finding "the right flowers to fit the right occasion," my sense of aesthetics called for a different artistic concept. There had to be another way to celebrate flowers with style, and I knew that this creative spark had begun to smolder inside me.

When I learned that fashion maverick Pierre Cardin was looking for a florist for his new shop Les Fleurs de Maxim's, I knew I had to have that job. With barely two francs to rub together, I found an electric blue Yves Saint Laurent suit on sale and went to meet Madame Renée Clément, the elegant director of the boutique. She asked for my résumé. I didn't have one. But Pierre Cardin interviewed me for more than an hour and gave me my chance. Fashion still inspires my work, and in my creations floral artistry and fashion design are closely related.

I spent the next eight years at Les Fleurs de Maxim's. On Rue Royale, one of the most beautiful and glamorous streets in the world, our clientele came from fashion, arts, high society, and show business—*Le Tout-Paris*. I never looked back to the sixteenth *arrondissement*. Surrounded by elegance, my eye encountered new trends, colors, and fabrics, and little by little I composed an artistic memory. I walked daily along the Jardin des Tuileries, through the majestic alleys of chestnut trees on the Champs-Élysées, and breathed in the beauty of Paris. I was inspired by the stunning architecture of the French capital, the lavish windows of the couturiers of Faubourg Saint-Honoré and Avenue Montaigne, and the glimmering creations of the jewelers of the Place Vendôme. I was home.

Madame Clément encouraged me to create original bouquets, and under her watchful eye, I felt liberated creatively. I admired her ease and skill with our demanding clients and was inspired by her impeccable taste. I was twenty-one when she put me in charge of styling our glamorous windows and shop, and her patient guidance helped me learn how to use a minimal space to maximum effect. One day Monsieur Cardin sent us a mannequin from his *maison de haute couture,* dressed in the most divine evening gown—the collar mimicked an exotic green leaf covered with sequins that wrapped graciously around the delicate neckline.

The impact of this amazing design has stayed with me to this day, and the exotic green leaf is still one of my signature touches. I began to see each window as a crucible, my own flower laboratory. I lined glass containers with exotic leaves of all sizes and colors, tied knots with leaves, and made leaves into bouquets. I freed them from their branches and allowed them to come out on their own. It was a revolution.

Les Fleurs de Maxim's had full access to the top flower vendors in the world, for the best quality and variety. One of our responsibilities was to flower Maxim's, the world-famous Belle Epoque restaurant conveniently located next door. For the first time, I could see the life of my arrangements after they left the shop. I sized up the history, the atmosphere, the décor, and was allowed to imagine what would complement the space to delight the customers and Maestro Cardin! Our arrangements shared the spotlight with Majorelle furniture, Massier vases, and Barbotine ceramics. I learned to add just the right touch to a décor or an art collection, to bring focus to an object and not to detract from it. My bouquets became a part of the scene in an organic way, they didn't steal the show. The sensual iris, emblematic of the Art Nouveau style, is still my favorite flower.

The boutique quickly became the most glamorous flower shop in town. When Barbra Streisand stayed at the Ritz, we sent enormous gardenia trees in full bloom; for Christina Onassis's wedding to Thierry Roussel, it was white phalaenopsis orchids cascading from the ceiling. On weekends I would scour flea markets for antique vases, accessories like feathers, and just about any object with a floral motif. While strolling through the stalls, inspired by my discoveries, I would construct wild new compositions in my head and then deconstruct them until I was satisfied with a final imaginary result. I still do this exercise daily, even on the subway.

When Pierre Cardin decided to open a new flower and perfume boutique in Tokyo, he sent me. The little spare time I had was spent filling my mind with new aesthetic experiences. My very French sensibilities were challenged by the unfamiliar. I wanted to travel to distant lands and I made it my priority to discover new destinations each year. An endless source of inspiration for my work, traveling still brings me great joy.

Soon it was on to New York City, where a new Maxim's restaurant opened on Madison Avenue with a tiny flower shop next door, re-creating artfully the Rue Royale scenario. I was promoted to director of the new boutique.

The shop was so small that Monty Zullo, the general manager of the restaurant, allowed me to use the restaurant as our atelier. I learned English, adapted to the American way of life, and very soon had more work than I'd ever dreamed. In the United States, I discovered a positive energy and an optimistic attitude, which I embraced.

In New York, I found that the sky is the only limit to all things creative. The extraordinary architecture, from the glass towers of Midtown to the industrial lofts of SoHo, inspired new ways to construct arrangements. The angles, dimensions, reflections, depths, and heights of this intense metropolis permeated my work.

I made many friends among designers, artists, photographers, writers, and musicians, and their talent inspires my work as well. Museums and galleries became the backdrop for many spirited discussions. I understood intuitively that New York's creative energy was fostered by an enthusiastic market. Collectors, art dealers, curators, patrons of the arts, benefactors, museums, cultural institutions are all hungry for and command works of value. I realized that a floral designer could go much further and that visual art could permeate my craft.

In 1992, Micky Palmer Boulud, the wife of restaurateur extraordinaire Daniel Boulud, stepped into the boutique. "I am working on my husband's first cookbook called *Cooking with Daniel Boulud,*" she said. "Could you help us display the ingredients for a photo shoot on a sixteen-feet-long by eight-feet-deep table? Can you do it?" she asked. Who could say no to displaying seafood, meats, fruits, vegetables, herbs, spices, and grains on a giant scale and making it all look as appetizing as it was aesthetically pleasing? This gigantic styling challenge would be carried out four times, once for each season. I was in.

The job did not require containers or flowers, my usual working tools. Instead I approached the task as an exercise in style. Diverse elements would be grouped to build a still life, a canvas of nature's seasonal bounty. As a Frenchman, I always had food as a central part of my life, and I relished the match. Fruits are the generous gifts of plants and trees, and flowers are often the symbols of rebirth and life. I extended into three dimensions the artistic tradition of the still life. The demanding chef was pleased with the results, and I have collaborated with him many times since. I now flower his New York restaurants, including his acclaimed four-star Daniel on Park Avenue.

In 1995, when an old bookstore went out of business on East 76th Street, Daniel Boulud called me. With the help of my extraordinary friend Lili Lynton, I was able to start my own business. L'Olivier Floral Atelier was born.

My day would start with an early visit to the flower market on 28th Street between 7th and 8th avenues. Each vendor on this magical New York street has a specialty: one offers the most beautiful cut flowers; another, exotic plants; a third, flowering branches. Tools, floral supplies, and unusual containers can be found there as well. I have developed strong relationships with my favorite suppliers, who will often set aside for me their most rare and prized items.

Thanks to the hard work and dedication of my team, we flower the homes of our loyal New York clientele, celebrate their weddings, birthdays, and anniversaries with our signature bouquets and arrangements. I strive to make them happy and enhance their lives with beauty. My generous clients often allow me to participate in other aspects of their lives as well: corporate events, product launches, the opening of restaurants, hotels, hair salons, offices, and even building lobbies. L'Olivier Floral Atelier is also proud to contribute to several charities and fund-raisers each year, such as Action Against Hunger, the Kips Bay Decorator Show House gala, New York City Ballet, Citymeals-on-Wheels, and the ASPCA.

Today, with two boutiques, numerous awards, and a wonderful family of clients, I strive to live surrounded by nature's most gorgeous achievements. From the gardens of Provence to my own New York terrace dedicated to Grand-Mère Lucie, I have painted my own artistic and professional landscape.

Come with me and meander through the interior gardens of some of my clients' special homes. I hope you will be touched and intrigued by my choices and that this book will ignite your creativity. Later thanks to technique and styling tips, we will make arrangements together.

Olivier

PART I

AT HOME

From small studios to large mansions, from classical style to contemporary design, flowers will enhance your surroundings. I invite you to follow me through a variety of residences to see some of the infinite number of possibilities available to you when flowering your home: bouquets tucked away in bookshelves, next to a stone hearth, on a kitchen counter, or perhaps on the marble floor of a powder room.

Why limit yourself to cut flowers in a vase? Expand your vision to include leaves, branches, field plants, grasses, succulents, cacti, and herbs. Each season will bring new treasures, as will visits to your local flower markets and nurseries.

For me the world is filled with objects that can be reborn as wonderful containers. Open your closets and use that antique ceramic tureen, a colored-glass bottle, a bamboo basket, or even the timeless piece of hollow driftwood the ocean dropped on your shore.

Don't be intimidated by the process. A creation can be as simple as a tray filled with sand, framed with seashells and topped by a plant resembling a starfish (see Kennedy, dining room table, page 46). In my recipes section, I will teach you the techniques behind such arrangements as round bouquets, centerpieces, and bathing calla lilies.

I hope this book will inspire you to flower your home regularly so you can experience the positive impact flowers and plants can have on your life. Let their unique beauty and inner joy transport you.

To this end, I flower many homes on a weekly basis. This process requires a close relationship with a client. At the beginning, I spend time in their homes and tour the rooms, learning about their lives, décor, and tastes. I absorb the space, lighting, general style, and atmosphere. Every piece of art, from homemade to museum worthy, intrigues me.

Which artifacts, furniture, and spaces will my arrangements best enhance? I visualize numbers, sizes, volume, color, texture, scent, and final impact by combining different options in my mind, until a satisfying image appears. The choice of vases and containers comes next, and I always prefer to work with the client's own. If the ideal vessel cannot be found, I supply some or start treasure-hunting around town.

The size, shape, material, and color of the container will help guide the choices for the bouquet itself. From antique to contemporary design, from handmade to industrial, containers and vases stretch the creative process. These indispensable objects must not only hold water and cradle flowers, in my floral philosophy they must also make a statement as ornamental pieces.

With the help of glass artists, I've designed many vases. Deborah Czeresko and I created a half-moon prune glass vase (see Huon, foyer, page 25) to host bathing calla lilies. With Jeffrey Goodman, we invented a line of bubble vases (see Kennedy, dining room table, page 46) inspired by Pierre Cardin's home in the South of France, and with James Heeley, we constructed square and rectangular mirrored containers for cut orchids (see Olivier's Apartment, media room, pages 198 and 199).

Choose a clear vase and you can play with its water level or color, add bubbles, and turn the water into gelatin. Show the stems and tie them elegantly together, or hide them and line the inside of the vase with a leaf. Clear vases can also play aquarium. I often make underwater compositions, stage the usual suspects—shells, starfish, seaweed, coral—immerse unexpected flowers, branches, and leaves. Opaque vases allow you to hide the construction materials—Oasis, chicken wire, or pebbles—necessary for shape.

Once you have settled on an appropriate container for your room, imagine the visual effect you are striving for. Focus on color, height, and volume. A trip to the flower market and its seasonal display will help narrow and define your choices.

Another option involves the use of artificial flowers and plants, available year-round. I am truly awed by the level of quality of these reproductions—sometimes it's almost impossible to unmask them—so why not mix these lovely impostors with the real thing? (See Guiliano, living room, page 112).

Though your chosen plants are safely nestled in the container, your job is not quite over. My finishing touch often includes embellishing the arrangement with some of my signature designs. With practice you, too, will come up with your own ideas.

For an organic and textured look, I line a large rectangular wood planter or "flat" with coconut bark to display a wheat field (see Huon, orange wheat field, page 28). For a tall vase, I tie a piece of cattail around its body to break the horizontal effect (see Kennedy, guest bedroom, page 55). I wrap an exotic leaf around a vase's neck to dress the flowers in a ruffle (see Olivier, red container with Brigitte Bardot, page 197). My cactus garden is planted in layers of sand, apparent through its clear square glass (see Daniel, page 137).

As you take a stroll through these living spaces, starting with the spectacular Howard residence on the following page, I hope you will let my flowers touch your heart and perhaps be inspired to bring your own visions to life.

THE HOWARD PENTHOUSE

One of the defining qualities of Lena and George Howard's penthouse, situated on the eighty-seventh floor of a glass tower in midtown Manhattan, is the *simple geometry* of the perfect *clean lines* that run throughout the home, allowing me to set the mood of each room with every floral arrangement I install. As soon as the front door opens, the stunning views pull you toward the *skyline* on the other side of the apartment.

In the foyer

(below) the visitor pauses for a moment, embraced by the warmth and colors of my native Provence. Four gray, transparent vases in a series hold sunflowers bound together with a thin hala leaf that serves as a living ribbon. The arrangements seem similar but each is made unique by the different way a second pointy hala leaf is placed and sculpted.

Behind the flowers, higher on the wall, hang two large monochromatic sunflower prints by contemporary Chinese artist Liu Dan. Mrs. Howard discovered him just before he burst onto the international art scene and commissioned several large-scale prints, enchanted by the delicacy of his modern calligraphy. By placing sunflowers in a sleek contemporary home floating above the harsh skyscrapers, I reinterpret their native context and transform them into urban accessories. Meandering through the South of France, we've all admired the striking sunflower fields immortalized by Van Gogh. As the Howards and their guests come and go through the foyer, they can carry with them a ray of beauty.

In the living room (opposite), looking at the round lamp, a paper sphere seemingly alive with pleats and crevices, I imagine the sun setting behind the city. Dotted with lighter gray circles, the silk pillows carry the circular theme along. Cymbidium orchids

9

and 'Jade' and 'Escimo' roses cut very short are arranged in floral foam spheres and plated on dark square trays (opposite top left and bottom right). Another tray offers vivacious and spiky faux osage oranges for a burst of color (opposite lower left). I strive not to distract from the stunning ancient horse sculptures but to enhance the coffee table and thus the whole living room.

Quince branches (below), can often be found as early as December, preceding the spring. Lily grass completes this snowy bouquet. In the window, two silver containers hold a forest of tender snowball viburnum (opposite top right).

As if to carry forward the long fresco (opposite) by artist Liu Dan, its thin Chinese calligraphy style brimming with sensual overtones, I brought the still flowers to life with 'Coral Charm' peonies, a symbol of spring.

The physical limitations of a vase do not curb my imagination, and I often let nature burst over boundaries, literally taking over. The cubes of different sizes that support the two arrangements allow the garland of jasmine to cascade softly over the stark console. Dan's contemporary interpretation of traditional Chinese peonies (above) inspired me not to replicate the painting but to expand on it thanks to a visual and tactile experience. The combination of jasmine with peonies can produce a sweet scent, perfectly suitable to a warm and inviting living room. Strands of horsetail and a thin fern leaf bind the living structure.

The long black-and-white triangles painted on Mrs. Howard's contemporary ceramic vases (page 15) seem to point to the twelve-foot-high ceiling

13

in the corner of the living room. Taking their lead, I decided to unroll the majestic corner like a vertical canvas.

Strong but always flexible, orange-painted bamboo poles set the stage for a long-lasting living sculpture, reminiscent of a giant Pan flute (opposite). I selected poles that were as tall as possible and cut them to different heights to evoke the ever-present Manhattan skyline. They are held together by yet another bamboo pole, sliced open, for a sharp contrast and a break in verticality.

To bring in depth and volume, I let the yellow 'James Story' orchids from Thailand burst out of the geometric vases, creating a multilayered arrangement. Behind them, I softened the ensemble by placing large fan leaves between the bamboos and the flowers. Long hala leaves are cut to just brush the floor and subdue the peaks and valleys of the vases.

On the gray side table, a glass-frosted green vase supports orange vanda orchids seeming to rest softly against a giant fan leaf. To mirror the antique rocking horse, I tied strands of horsetail stems in a long grassy ponytail.

Dinner is about to be served. The menu? French, of course.

Suspended above the scintillating city, a black dining room table seems to float above the earth and under the white fluorescent sails of the Cubist hanging light fixture.

For this French dinner, Mrs. Howard has chosen evocative Bernardaud plates from La Collection d'Agnès Thurnauer. The name of a painting, picked by the artist from among the most famous paintings in the world, adorns each plate. To balance *Mona Lisa* and *Le déjeuner sur l'herbe,* I selected my own kind of masterpiece, the green cymbidium orchid, featured in four centerpieces. Square dark platters hold orchids set as low as possible, allowing the guests to see each other. Next to the flowers, a soft dune covered with moss hints at a Japanese garden. To create an ensemble and a link between the four vases, stems of horsetail make an organic path. Each centerpiece also features two horsetail strands bent to represent a bridge, symbol of peaceful communication. Instead of a napkin ring, a strand of variegated lily grass is looped around each napkin, bearing one blossom of green cymbidium orchid.

On the console, standing next to the antique Chinese sculptures, I placed straight horsetail stems of different lengths in dark oval vases. This transparent curtain is my interpretation of the luminescent skyline. ■

THE HUON COUNTRY HOUSE

Half hidden in the thick Cold Spring forest, fashion executive Jean Claude Huon's home resembles a miniature Frank Lloyd Wright Fallingwater with its *stone* and *wood* exterior and a cascade running along its side. *Water* seems to flow throughout the trilevel house and was the source of my inspiration.

In the foyer, I was transported by the wonderful photograph depicting a hothouse for water lilies in Holland, and chose blue and lavender hyacinths to bring out the colors of the picture. As soon as the door opens, the flowers' springy fragrance fills the air—a lovely welcome. To allow enough space between the flowers and the frame, so as not to detract from the art but enhance it, the hyacinths are nestled within two low, half-moon plum vases I designed (below). My trademark leaves nod to the water lilies in the picture: I sculpted both broad alocasia leaves and bear grass. Another leaf is bent and molded inside the vase, allowing its veins to show and bringing depth to the base of the arrangement.

In my world, leaves are not meant to fill space or be treated as filler, they are an integral part of my living sculptures.

The heart of this all-season weekend house lies at the center of its sunken living room. From the carved-rock hearth the light of the fire is reflected on the wooden table.

I created a long-lasting, organic sculpture from a series of sinewy dried and bleached grapevines dancing by the fireplace (page 24). They remind me of my childhood and the smooth branches I once gathered along the banks of the Rhône. Touching the stone, the branches unfurl beyond the boundaries of the vase.

On the coffee table, I bring more fire to the underlying current of rock, wood, and water: 'Flaming Parrot' tulips, supported by a philodendron leaf wrapped around the stems (opposite). A Gymea leaf bridges to a bouquet of delicate orange asclepias.

On the table, three L'Olivier candles, created for me by James Heeley, mix their own unique scent—a blend of jasmine, tuberose, lily of the valley, and violet—to the burning wood.

What better way to spend a weekend morning than reading while comfortably ensconced in the Womb Chair? For this quiet corner, I imagined a field of painted orange wheat playing off the William Morris Machado paintings and the fiery chair (opposite). Embedded in a low rectangular vase covered with coconut fiber, the wheat eases the transition from the countryside to the more urban Knoll leather chaise.

The stunning Bernardaud vase—a tower of plates stacked slightly off center from one another—supports agile poppies as if held by the hand of a fantastic maître d' (below left). I love to use the medium of my floral sculptures to fuse artistic genres: winding stems hold a black and red croton leaf and dance out of the white structure, furthering the illusion of movement.

A week later, I would have created a completely different arrangement. But on that cool spring day, the trees surrounding the house were still bare, their lacy limbs reflecting on the tranquil surface of the Knoll table, as if a section of the frozen lake had moved indoors.

In keeping with the 1970s theme coursing through the house, I chose globelike vases and placed round mirrors of different sizes under the plants and the candle holders to accentuate the reflective quality (opposite). The black irises, one of my favorite flowers, fit within the aquatic landscape and call to mind the butterfly chair on the deck (below).

Akin to an indoor weeping willow, this majestic six-foot tree trunk (page 32) hints at the real specimen on the other side of the lake. I built this organic sculpture to inhabit the corner of the dining room and blur the lines between the jagged out-doors and the refined interior space.

At the peak of the trunk, weeping willow branches share the spotlight with aquatic heads of papyrus for a natural, unpolished look (opposite).

I often find my most powerful inspiration in the simplest of places, like the earth tones of an old wood floor, from which grew this mighty indoor tree.

The imposing curvaceous Japanese console dominates the landing between floors and makes you pause. The curled legs remind me of polished branches as I will them to metamorphose into a living pedestal for my fantasy Japanese garden.

I admire the innate elegance of this ancient cluster of sequoia bonsai, still standing tall, an unlikely survivor of a devastating forest fire (below left). On the forest floor, life slowly reappears in the form of bright green moss. Perfumed wooden spheres from L'Artisan Parfumeur lead to an oncidium orchid plant leaning against an elongated slice of coconut boat.

In the whimsical guest room, a long side-table functions as a nightstand. I placed two fantastic Michael Vollbracht collages and an African mask as a backdrop to the simple but vibrant bouquet of red arachnis orchids, accentuated by a Gymea leaf (below right). Batman, one of my childhood heroes, keeps vigil over the wooden snake. ■

With her warm personality, it is no wonder that friends hold a special place in the heart of the prominent journalist whose apartment contains this sumptuous dining room, perfect for entertaining. I recently had the pleasure of helping her throw an autumn birthday party for one of her closest girlfriends. That day, this gorgeous Manhattan apartment summoned forth the warm breezes and scents of sunny Florida. We had been inspired by a lovely black-and-white photograph taken in Palm Beach of the birthday girl as a young lady, in which she gazes through an elegant wrought-iron gate as if into the future. This image gave rise to a fantasy patio landscape.

A screen made of wrought-iron leaves frames the décor and supports anthurium leaves and succulent plants while tall Kentia palms whisper a tropical song.

On the tables I design for events, a single signature centerpiece often incorporates a multitude of smaller parts. In my imaginary Floridian patio, silvery pink, 'Green Fashion', and 'Black Beauty' roses share the stage with light pink and green cymbidium orchids and red and white astilbes (page 35). Mixing seasonal fruits and berries, I specifically chose pomegranate branches, symbols of longevity. I learned early on that well-chosen flowers enhance conversation and inspire warmth and harmony at the table. ■

THE KENNEDY BEACH HOUSE

A few steps away, Shinnecock Bay shimmers in the summer light. This 1915 Hampton Bays weekend home belongs to Judith Curr, a busy publishing executive, and her husband, architect Ken Kennedy. They come to their *beach house* year-round, to breathe in the silver light of the ocean and leave their urban stresses behind. The house is a *peaceful haven* where Ms. Curr can read through manuscripts uninterrupted. The old Hamptons shingles offer a counterpoint to the *modern interior*, a creative mix of West Coast meets Scandinavian design.

I have always loved the lines of the 1950s Modern style, so I used the clean-cut George Nelson bench as a table in the house's enclosed veranda to support the two colorful and informal *boules* vases I designed. In the blue one, garlic scapes—which I love for their poetically twisted stems—curl toward a tight bunch of hot-pink carnations, an often undervalued and affordable flower. On the shelf, a piece of driftwood smoothed by sea and sand holds allium pods. I often fill old pieces of hollow wood with new growth, a symbol of renewal and hope.

The moment I set foot in the festive living room, my eye immediately went to the bicolor geometric rug and its unusual color combination (opposite bottom). Because I consider hydrangeas to be the symbol of the Hamptons, I filled the room with large, hand-tied bouquets of 'You and Me Together', 'Vendetta Lavender', and 'Magical Opal' cultivars, cradled by large philodendron leaves. On one end of the coffee table, an exuberant bouquet of clematis and hosta leaves balances a low arrangement of vanda orchids. When placing flowers on a coffee table, it's important to use low arrangements to allow guests to see each other.

The corner of the room cradles elongated branches of Sumbawa wood that mirror the vertical lines of the painting and remind me of long Giacometti figures.

In this perspective, I show three different but equally effective ways to present flowers. In the corner, a large philodendron leaf acts as a ribbon and lets the flowers burst above it (opposite top right). The different hues provide nuance as I paint a natural indigo landscape. In the middle, a seemingly simple hosta leaf anchors a clematis bouquet and defies gravity as it inches toward the lower side of a sloped glass vase. Dieffenbachia leaves create a bed for a branch of vanda orchids leaning away from the boundaries of the container and toward the front of the room (opposite top left).

I am often asked how many flowers make the perfect arrangement. As in this opulent bouquet of hydrangeas, my answer lies not within the space constraints of the container but within the room as a whole. In this case, the width of the table becomes the basis for the composition, letting the size and importance of the vase recede.

The entire space becomes the canvas, and the choices I make must give a sense of unity to it; color and texture, the height and depth all become brushstrokes to achieve the feeling of completeness.

In times past, a Renaissance ruffled collar would have been the necessary detail to complete an outfit. Today, remembering Pierre Cardin's touch, I fashion a wide hosta leaf as a collar to round out a swirl of blue clematis, simply resting on the side of the glass vase (opposite).

I strongly believe that every single part of a plant is worth displaying. The flowers are, of course, its apotheosis. But don't disregard the stem, its foundation and sturdy companion.

By tying the stems in this arrangement with my signature leafy knot, I bring attention to the lower part of the bouquet, extending the viewer's pleasure.

Visible through the floor-to-ceiling window, branches and shrubs enter the room like a living tableau. I wanted the long-lasting burst of 'White Feather' pampas grass with livistona leaves to balance the white hanging lamp fixture and soften the corner where a woman at work has just left the room (opposite top).

On the dining table, a natural, varied garden of plants, flowers, and objects keeps her company. The beach house theme and assortment of low bubble vases unite the ensemble. I saw the tabletop as a reflection of her surroundings, a continuation of her garden by the bay.

I designed these bubble vases, handblown by Jeff Goodman, as a collection inspired by Pierre Cardin's 1954 iconic bubble dresses. They work particularly well with long-stemmed flowers like the tall lavender with lamb's ears at the base, or the creamy 'Mount Everest' allium in the pale green container (opposite).

Two separate bouquets in the same vase take advantage of the low aperture. The blue and purple brodea display their own character, each bunch pointing in a different direction. I emphasize the aura of the shore with shells, sand, and blue echeveria succulent plants, all served on a rattan platter (opposite bottom).

Flowers provide infinite variety of color and texture. Playfully experimenting with lines and height, I strive for the ideal composition, the perfect balance.

Bouquets can be as simple and as poetic as a vertical living structure made from strands of allium, a delicate flower of the common onion family.

Since the stems of lavender are so thin, it is best to fit as many as possible in the low bubble vases so they will stand tall. But I left some slivers of space for the lamb's ear leaves to help the transition between glass and flowers (opposite).

The intoxicating scent and iridescence of lavender always takes me back to the Provençal *garrigues* of my youth.

Arrangements that at first appear simple actually offer both yin and yang, one of the dichotomies of nature I admire the most. Opposite the shells and sand that I just gathered from the beach, I placed an echeveria succulent plant, juxtaposing its water-filled leaves with the dry grainy beauty of the shore.

The appearance of simplicity—despite hours of planning and often painstaking execution—is a goal in itself. I adore Mozart, whose genius makes the complex seem easy. When an installation succeeds, it achieves a kind of rightness. These elements are in perfect proportion in space and time and achieve a harmony beyond the moment.

Variations in texture can be as important as variations in color. Thinly rolled smooth alocasia leaves cover the spiny globe thistle and prickly *Trifolium alpinum* for an original look (page 47).

From this calm perch above field and ocean, a blue bedroom with a view (below), manuscripts come to life as the reader winds through the pages. I chose to let the view and outdoor vegetation shine and become the focal point. Simple touches, such as thin strands of cattails and heavily textured *Begonia masoniana* leaves on the floating nightstand, create a sophisticated balance.

I tell the story of a couple by picking different varieties of flowers or plants for each side of the bed. The lady's side features delicate and feminine hydrangeas, resembling a cloud of butterflies. On the gentleman's side, spiny, prickly thistles

float on a large philodendron leaf. I love their combination of purple spikes and velvet hearts.

For this tableau, torn between the strong blue of the lamps and the white wall expanse, I chose to amplify the dark side and selected deep blue cobalt vases (opposite top left).

Flowers can have many meanings, and the best way to approach a bedroom is to allow the flowers to breathe and blend into the décor, without making too loud a statement.

The use of mirrors in decoration needs to be carefully thought through. I focused on the color yellow jumping out at me from the bright Sydney Opera poster across the room and matched it with the extravagant hanging 'She Kong' heliconia, which I ran along the length of the vase (opposite lower left). A rush of oncidium orchids, wrapped with philodendron and often called 'Dancing Ladies' for their lovely contour (opposite top right), occupy a large portion of the mirror. I love working with yellow, symbol of the sun, as it brightens both my day and any room.

A small ceramic container holds asparagus ferns (opposite lower right), calling to mind a low forest of pine trees and balancing the exuberance of the taller creation.

I remember seeing many bamboo and cane pieces of furniture in my travels throughout Asia and thought that this five-foot Chinese vase would feel right at home in the guest room.

The corner of a room, especially if there's a window, can often lend itself to a large arrangement. Such height as I found here called for tall flowers such as hybrid delphiniums, which I picked in blue, purple, and white, the colors I associate most with a beach landscape. I treasure the scent of eucalyptus leaves, a lemony impression reminiscent of Mediterranean shores. The large philodendron leaves dress up the vase, finishing its organic costume (below).

Long cattails resembling bamboo posts embrace the Chinese forest painted on the vase (opposite). I let the stems escape from the ceramic canvas and into our reality. ■

THE PRE-WAR SURFING
PHOTOGRAPHS OF DON JAMES
LY 1 TO AUGUST 14, 1998
NZIGER GALLERY
1 MADISON AVENUE
EW YORK 10021

160

The fantastic underwater world created by Sherri and Peter Venokur in the kitchen of their Flatiron loft inspired me to expand on the coral mosaic of the walls and paint my own version of a *20,000 Leagues Under the Sea* décor—complete with shells, sea urchins, pincushion flowers, and an orange fish swimming along in the aquarium.

Next to the stove, ruby red–painted manzanita branches undulate in front of the mosaic tiles. At the base, I suggest a seaweed underbrush with red holiday cactus flowers and leaves bursting out of a shimmering metallic vase.

I envisioned the Hall of Ocean Life at the American Museum of Natural History and approached the arrangement on the breakfast counter like a painting, using a full palette of color, object, and texture to express myself. Orange protea play the role of the anemone, hugging the reef while succulent plants and trachelium share the spotlight with an array of shells. A long transparent vase containing an aspidistra leaf and an aquatic plant is inserted into the fishbowl for a fun goggle effect.

On the top shelf of the pantry, in front of a plate where Oriental fish twirl joyously, I let two bundles of mango calla lilies languidly bathe their long legs (opposite bottom). Two short philodendron stems encase the bouquets and aspidistra leaves wrapped around the ends bring an elegant finale to the ensemble. A pavé of pincushions alludes to the retro feel of the popcorn popper (opposite top). ■

THE LICHTBLAU RESIDENCE

THE LICHTBLAU RESIDENCE

A gorgeous spring *light* filters through the towering circular French doors of Anne and George J. Lichtblau's dreamy New Canaan, Connecticut, rotunda (opposite), the perfect setting for an *elegant* afternoon tea. A trellislike cachepot holds a bouquet of spring peonies peppered with green viburnum wrapped in a philodendron leaf. Ornamental pineapples in various *shades of pink* grow into a cheerful leitmotif for the room. Mixed with mini sago palm leaves, they occupy two antique Chinese planters placed on pedestals, framing the monumental doors to the garden and natural pond. Playing against expectations, I add even more height to the space, inviting a visitor to follow the lines of the plants to the soaring dome above.

On each level of the three-tiered gueridon, temptingly colored delicacies are juxtaposed with flowers and plants of different heights (opposite). On a nearby console, a crystal vase holds yellow ornithogalum while another vase

cradles white calla lilies, orange ranunculus, and geranium leaves (above). My definition of teatime abundance: each tray carries an array of colors, tastes, and depth—calla lilies surrounded by mint-scented geranium leaves, mini pineapples, and ruby red cherries; luscious lemon and apricot macaroons remind me of Paris and lie alongside yellow and orange ranunculus; white Majolica spray roses, lemon madeleines (the ideal French cookie), perfectly shaped kumquats, and hosta leaves support more mini pineapples.

When Mr. and Mrs. Lichtblau moved into their colonial house, they discovered an antique bathtub with delicate leaves painted onto the porcelain (below). Mrs. Lichtblau's keen eye immediately saw the whimsical accent the piece could bring to their new breakfast room. Today, it seems to have been created only to hold a garden of orchids. I reprised Mrs. Lichtblau's favorite hues and nestled two watering cans among leaves and moss for an original look. As if the water had been left on too long, branches of English ivy and Boston fern overflow into the room.

Guests are on their way, and under the exquisite chandelier, Cristal Champagne is ready to be poured. The inlaid table supports delicate Yves Delorme crystal vases with mini purple phalaenopsis and blue vanda orchids, as well as Vermeer calla lilies surrounded by lily grass loops (opposite bottom left).

Letting the Chinese-accented wallpaper and custom-made English furniture lead my inspiration toward the Far East, I set the dining room to evoke exotic lands and a globe-trotting spirit. I recall a trip to Kyoto, where peaceful gardens and simple bouquets brought forth my inner energy.

Classic candelabra balance the marble-top console where a mane of pink phalaenopsis orchids envelops a Baccarat vessel lined with my signature philodendron leaf (opposite top left). I sculpted strands of lily grass in another Baccarat vase for added depth and transparency (opposite bottom left).

I see the orchid as the most sophisticated flower; intricate and simple in the same breath, holding the essence of beauty in its delicate petals.

On the western wall of the dining room, leaves speak as loudly as blossoms. I worship the leaf. For me the noble leaf exults and uplifts the flower, as essential as yin to yang. A silver urn holds lamb's ears and dusty miller chosen for their soft tint and velvety feel (opposite bottom right).

In the radiant archway that leads to the new wing (opposite), two country-chic consoles support opulent bouquets of pink, green, and blue popcorn hydrangeas (below) leaning against lush eucalyptus foliage. A eucalyptus branch is embossed in the Yves Delorme clear vases. Here I recall my youthful jaunts in Provence, where bushy leaves give contrast to even the largest of blossoms.

I love the antique Chinese medicine doll, often used by elegant and modest ladies to indicate to their doctors (usually men) the part of their body where they were experiencing pain or discomfort.

After working for years in the haute couture world of Pierre Cardin, I am totally at home adding a special touch to a lady's boudoir. I complete this feminine universe—a favorite cream-colored gardenia-clad Chanel purse, a just-discarded mauve jacket, and a pair of Manolos—with two different-colored freesias in Anne Lichtblau's favorite hues, shocking pink and purple (opposite). I relish the sweet scent of freesias, a fresh perfumed note but not so strong as to overpower the jasmine essence of Chanel's Coco.

The Chinese carved pink jade vase (above) provides the perfect vessel, delicate but sturdy, and the curvature of the flower clusters balances the strong lines of the room. ▨

THE GREY LOFT

How does one complement the formidable talent of Joel Grey?
For the singer/actor/dancer/photographer, art doesn't just belong
on the walls or on the stage, it informs every part of his home.
Joel has transformed an industrial loft overlooking the Hudson

River into a collector's home,
featuring unique and refined
pieces. His ability as a curator
comes forth in the quality and
originality of the objects that
surround him as well as his
unusual choice of materials, such
as concrete for ceilings, walls,
and floors. My challenge was to
let his style prevail but enhance
the exhibition space.

With a long Plexiglas vase set on the dining table, I solved the issue of transparency and then simply slid tall white calla lilies against one side of the container. The vase also alludes to Robert Rauschenberg's nearby Plexiglas installation.

In the sleek concrete bathroom, I noticed a sepia photograph of a little boy standing in a forest of giant lilies of the valley. This picture intrigued me and I asked Joel about it. In fact, this is a collage he created. He cut out a picture of himself as a child, glued it on a photo of a field full of lilies of the valley, and then shot a photograph of the collage. Joel remembers growing up in the suburbs of Cleveland, Ohio, and wandering alone in a wooded area near his parents' house. His favorite thing was "finding a precious patch of lily of the valley, perfect in design, so fragile, yet so sturdy and with a fragrance that made the larger flowers weep with envy."

His passion for this particularly delicate flower as well as its sweet aroma led him to create this fantasy landscape, his own version of a safe and beautiful haven. As an homage to the little boy, I placed a window box of lilies of the valley on the side of the tub for a deliciously fragrant bath (opposite). In the living room, an antique Louis Vuitton trunk displays an eclectic and charming array of sculptures and artifacts (above). Among them I placed long eucharis, white tulips, and ethereal feather reed grass. The stage is set. ▪

THE LEIBA DUPLEX

For me, stepping into Freddie Leiba's apartment is akin to taking a *journey* around the world. Born in Trinidad and reared in London, the talented stylist and editor explores distant shores for his clients and often brings back *exotic* treasures for his own Upper West Side pad. Freddie encouraged me to search the closets for unique containers, which I mixed fearlessly for a *baroque* assemblage.

I have been a fortunate guest at many parties here and opted to re-create with plants and flowers the kind of ethnic buffet my host lovingly prepares for his friends. Illustrious Albert Watson's photograph of a young Moroccan snake charmer (opposite top left) reminds me of the bazaar in Marrakech's Djemaa el Fna square, a fascinating and bustling center of humanity.

Framed by gracious arches of areca palms, the dining room table offers a rich array of fruits and tropical plants such as fig branches, a monumental black banana cluster with its pointy reddish flower still attached, and towering red heliconia, also known as lobster claws.

Who says a baroque soup terrine cannot become a perfect vessel for a flower arrangement (opposite bottom left)? Shapely purple vanda and pink and green cymbidium orchids lie alongside a twist of straight steelgrass. The grass stems are so sturdy that they stand straight without support. I love mixing the purity of their verticality with the elaborate rococo orchids.

We might all harbor a primal fear of snakes, but I think we cannot deny their beauty and the perfection of their shape. The boy's intense stare inspires respect, so I paid homage to his bravery with a cobra-shaped candlestick as well as a python-skin runner placed on the table (opposite bottom right).

I chose the bicolor wooden vase with a tiger pattern to hold a leaning bouquet of white tuberoses. I find their sweet scent delicious and uplifting. To complete the design (opposite top right), I add my signature knotted bicolor hala leaves to the base of the flowers. By placing the vase close to the python runner, I add a touch of Africa to the scene. I always try to draw on my travels to varied corners of the globe to inform and extend my creations.

In the foyer, a mirrored wall over the console reflects black-and-white photographs of antique Roman and Greek sculptures (opposite). The expanse of the mirror called for something that would literally stand up to its multidimensionality. A tall arrangement of blue hybrid delphinium, deep hued and elegant, provides the intense complement to the color of the wall. Memories of past summer pilgrimages transported me to the cradle of antiquity; the Mediterranean atmosphere gains dimension from the long fig tree branch.

A defiant Masai warrior defends his domain: the bookshelf, peppered with exotic artifacts and travel books. I paint an African jungle around him, from the bromeliads and green hanging amaranthus at the roof level to papyrus stems (opposite bottom left), my interpretation of trees. To these I add various tones of red found in the ginger torches and the protuberant calatheas closer to the bottom (opposite top right). On the floor, cream tree peonies radiate their soft scent (opposite top left). By inviting sculptural elements into my scenes, I can expand on the floral vocabulary and invite a dialogue between culture and beauty.

On the console in the entrance (below), I dressed pavés of multicolor celosias in coconut skin, while figs and green lady slipper orchids rest in a bowl.

Lucky guests will wake up in this African bedroom with its raffia wallpaper and evocative paintings (opposite). In the pleated sarongs, I see giant tropical leaves. The face of a woman, carved from a Moroccan tree trunk planted with hanging heliconia, looks dreamily toward the window.

North Africa, with its traveling horsemen and sleepy kasbah, were my lodestones for the master bedroom. I love to visit Morocco, a gorgeous and enchanted land of multicolored light. With this in mind, I combine yellow oncidium orchids—a favorite sun symbol—with branches of olive trees, icons of peace. ▪

High above the hustle and bustle of Park Avenue hides a romantic and feminine Upper East Side haven. Owned by Georgette Farkas, perhaps the finest public relations executive in the culinary world, the apartment exudes her favorite period: 18th-century France. The Francophile soul of the owner is visible everywhere, from the bust of Marie-Antoinette to a *boule*-style desk inherited from an adored grandfather and an Aubusson rug found at an auction. I love spaces that make me feel like a time traveler or a voyager to a different land.

Seen through the luxurious drapes and old-fashioned French doors, a large terrace surrounds the apartment and adds a greenhouse element. From the terrace, I pick plum branches and white scabiosa and plant an imaginary Petit Trianon garden around the elegant sculpture. Vaporous purple smoke bush and pink asclepias bring more femininity to the tableau. To accentuate the steps leading to the outdoors, I place bouquets of oak leaves and hydrangeas at various heights to paint an interior landscape. The aroma of the geranium leaves at the bottom of the silver vase adds a sweet touch surrounding the white scabiosa. Plum

tree branches planted in a two-foot-high silver flute give the illusion of a tree and add depth and color.

On the desk, a silver champagne bucket holds Majolica spray roses 'Juliet', 'Miranda', and 'Judy' old garden roses (opposite). It is a joy to bring timeless floral decorations to such an elegant space.

It is possible to live in the center of Manhattan and spend time gardening. No matter how busy she gets, Ms. Farkas can always find a little time to relax on her wraparound terrace (left), above the fast-paced city. Together we designed the outdoor space to reflect a northeastern garden, showcasing her favorite trees, shrubs, foliage, and flowers. A few cast-iron chairs and tables are arranged to take advantage of the unparalleled sunset and sunrise views over the city's rooftops. She takes great pleasure in watching the mountain laurel bloom and tending to her roses, and then enjoys using the results of her labor in the beautiful bouquets that enliven her interior space.

Here, after a light spring shower, I assembled for the living room a bouquet of mountain laurel, asclepias, 'Juliet' garden roses, and cream hydrangea. ∎

THE ANDERSON PIED-A-TERRE

THE ANDERSON PIED-A-TERRE

Is this New York or Paris? I was seduced by the elegance of this discreet town house on one of Manhattan's most stately tree-lined streets. Behind its patrician facade there lies a 1930s studio—a *starch-white*, true *atelier d'artiste* owned by architect and interior decorator Jack Anderson. Several distinct areas are connected by his superb taste and passion for *French Art Deco* objects, art, and furniture.

In front of Man Ray's 1926 portrait "Noire et Blanche" on the mirrored console, I created my own mirror image with two contrasting bouquets (page 98). In the black vase, velvety 'Schwarzwalder' calla lilies seem to reflect the portrait's 1920s, ebony, slicked-back style. The peach vase holds 'Crystal Blush' calla lilies, always sought after for their pearly white hue. Only the roundness of the vases, a shape that is highlighted and extended through the sculpted stems, provides a visual counterpoint to the angular lines.

Jack Anderson and I are artistic soul mates. Jack composes with furniture and objects, and I work with flowers and plants, but both our lives are dedicated to beauty and to our personal craft, with the ultimate goal of improving a room, a home, the world.

It can be tempting to break a monochromatic theme with a strong colorful anchor. In this case, I opt for peaceful harmony and select white Oriental 'Rio Blanca' lilies and yucca leaves in white ceramic vases. The fan shape of the bouquet reflects the A-line of the pedestals (page 101).

Antique wooden pedestals remind me of the opera *La Bohème*. I imagine them in the artist's atelier, the loyal friends who support the sculptures and the canvases. Witness to the process of creation, they now deserve the purest, whitest arrangement, to perhaps transport the viewer to a more perfect world.

White 'Super Parrot' tulips with their green and white frills are among the largest in the tulip family (opposite). Next to the rolled bicolor hosta leaves, they make a gorgeous ensemble. Rectangles can seem strict, but I follow their lines for purity and symmetry. Here I treat the fireplace and the mirror as imaginary windows to the outdoors.

A simple, modernist fireplace supports three different arrangements, an assorted trio (opposite). The first two vases, one vertical rectangle and one horizontal, feature white 'Maureen' tulips of different heights. The third, placed strategically in front of the stems, contains an array of paperwhite narcissus bulbs. I enjoy working with bulbs for their organic feel, their earthy tones, and the living promise they carry.

From afar, the two vases holding tulips appear linear and orderly. This close-up reveals the innate chaos of nature; stems and leaves fight for space and air as they take center stage on the stark mantel.

On the floor, inspired by its country garden aura, I fill the cast-iron container with a cluster of white daisies, bringing a field of spring to this intensely urban apartment.

Layers of materials and multidimensionality come together to achieve an utter simplicity in this scene. As if on a balcony, white daisy plants are held together by a railing of dark bamboo, stretching toward the sky. I know I have achieved the desired impact when the appearance of simplicity emerges from highly complex objects—as if there could be no other way for them to be assembled.

Atop the stereo cabinet, mini pale yellow phalaenopsis orchids spring out of a small sculpted vase. Notice the face within the vase (above left)—it seems carved on a tree trunk, as if the whole arrangement were an organic living creature.

Nearby, spongy green moss breathes through the round windows dotting the sides of two little pots (opposite bottom). As if growing from a soft meadow, more pale yellow phalaenopsis reach their tranquil arms toward the sunlight.

On the Jean-Michel Frank desk, everything is set for an intense day of study. Objects lend their purpose to a symmetrical tableau. Two vases hold fans of carnivorous sarracenia known for their lacy, frilly petals and held by a philodendron stem, made to reflect the waterline while holding the flowers in place (opposite top).

The enigmatic mouth from Man Ray's 1966 "Kiki's Lips" (opposite) watches over the bed like a modern *Mona Lisa* and conveys an explosion of red eroticism, despite the photograph's black-and-white constraints. I responded to that invitation with three ripe and plump 'Red Charm' peonies, allowing their petals to reach beyond the confines of the earthenware vase. The red-covered book, *Erotic Drawings*, completes an explicit but exquisite tableau. ■

Mireille Guiliano, the celebrated and chic author of *French Women Don't Get Fat*, may have spent years at the helm of Veuve Clicquot, the celebrated Champagne company founded in 1772, but she appreciates modern surroundings and original style as much as quiet elegance.

Inspired by the thin circular staircase curling inside Ms. Guiliano's duplex in Chelsea, I mirrored the movement with an upside-down organic tower set in black river stones (bottom right). The cylinder of light streaming through the window falls on more than twenty "boats" made from coconut bark mixed with aspidistra leaves attached to a steel pole.

Elegant minimalism and serenity reign in the living room, where a long gray ceramic bottle supports faux agave leaves I molded and knotted to resemble a whimsical scarf. On the coffee table, three separate bouquets—'Libretto' and 'Apricot Parrot' tulips adorned with arrows made of hala leaves—lie sideways in a transparent vase (opposite). I tied each with two levels of silver wire to resemble African bracelets, which bring out the modern silver feet of the table. By using the wire to wrap the stems, I indulge another aspect of my artistic vision: the crisp geometric lines of the green stems form an ideal contrast to the open petals. ■

THE CARROLL HOME

THE CARROLL HOME

When Constance and Michael Carroll decided to sell their beloved vacation house in the South of France near Toulouse, they brought home enough furniture and objects to re-create an elegant *French country* atmosphere in their sprawling Connecticut family mansion. A delicious scent of lilac welcomes the visitor as soon as the door opens. Step under the cathedral ceiling of the foyer, where Andy Warhol's *lavish* and *sensuous* silkscreen portrait of Marilyn Monroe offers the perfect backdrop for an explosion of purple spring as lilacs soar from a terra-cotta urn. I accentuated the full lips, the strong eye shadow, and the whole Pop Art palette of colors with a plump, rust-tone porcelain pigeon from Toulouse.

In the foyer, I followed the noble iron curls of the console legs and

created a sense of movement thanks to lascivious strands of English ivy, reminiscent of a vine-covered French *maison de campagne*. Touches of dried moss in small antique terra-cotta vases add more hints of nature.

Though the front door marks the clear frontier between the garden and the interior of this cozy home, I longed to stretch nature's bounty into the foyer. Outside, the path is lined with low boxwood, a pattern I extended inside, with moss laid

in an ancient terra-cotta urn (opposite). From this angle, the lush spring lilacs laced with English ivy appear to be not a bouquet, but a shrub growing on the elegant console.

I love Paris. While at Les Fleurs de Maxim's, I often strolled from Rue Royale to Place de la Concorde gorging on the beauty of the square. To bring Alexander Vethers's stunning black-and-white photograph of the central fountain to life, I surrounded it with topiaries, the sort often found around ancient springs.

119

Framed by two preserved spiral boxwoods emerging proudly out of Chambord vases, an antique cast-iron console is supported by sinewy feet evoking mysterious stems.

I selected spheres of moss (left) to re-create the feeling and musty scents of a century-old stone fountain and peppered the scene with pictures of the oldest and youngest daughters in the family. Antique terra-cotta pots hold mini olive trees, santolina, and myrtle plants (opposite). A garland of boxwood underlines this elegant tableau like a hedge.

The balance between color and dimension is always an exercise in moderation, so I chose to keep the wonderful photograph as the focal point, letting it be enhanced but not overpowered by the textures of the garden.

On the magnificent painted dresser with its long, leafy garland, I positioned a bouquet of orange *Fritillaria imperialis* chosen for its regal, pendulum-style flower (opposite)—a wink to the candlesticks—but also for the thin leaves that grow vertically from the flowers. A large philodendron leaf eases the transition from stone to stem, and thin blades of lily grass swell over the Medici vase.

In this French country–style, open kitchen and dining room, I relive my Provençal childhood. Our feast is set on the antique farm table, and the cheese and wine party is about to start. The stout ceramic artichokes holding court on the dresser sparked my imagination for the centerpiece, as I gathered young purple artichokes and surrounded them with strands of rosemary on a stone gravel runner (opposite). On either side, bouquets of 'Sterling Silver' roses in similar terra-cotta pots extend the theme and the color palette.

Green hellebores, their flowers mimicking delicate leaves, seem ripe for picking, and on the cheese plate, purple blackberries appear as fantasy artichokes in miniature. I chose roses with no scent to let the aroma of the nearby herb garden and the rosemary on the napkin take precedence. On the dresser, 'Ocean Song' roses and hydrangeas mixed with delicate English ivy mirror the country-style spread.

Need to pluck a sprig of thyme or mint for that perfect Bocuse lamb recipe? I felt completely at home in this epitome of a French country kitchen (opposite top). As is often done in Provence, I planted an ornamental herb garden. Hidden within the miniature forest, a wisteria branch speaks of summer meals on the veranda. A metal flower box complements the kitchen accessories and chef's stove (opposite bottom). On the counter, an antique terra-cotta urn holds an aromatic bouquet of rosemary; a well-worn casserole plays fruit bowl, as giant artichokes, cherry tomatoes, and artisanal olive oils with their sunny shadows contribute to an elegant and familiar bucolic spirit.

To me, Audrey Hepburn symbolizes the perfect mix of innocence and elegance (opposite). Soft pastel colors surround eleven-year-old Eleanor's enchanting bedroom, in which I arranged a cluster of lavender, cream, pink, and fuchsia sweet peas. A stream of English ivy brushes up against the hand-painted dresser, adding another dimension to its delicate, leafy design (below).

This very feminine bathroom (opposite) reminds me of Versailles and Marie-Antoinette's beloved Petit Trianon, where I would often take long walks while I lived in Paris. The French faience tiles lining the walls serve as a backdrop for this noble lady, just back from picking roses in her garden. At her feet, I lay a delightful rosebush cradled in an elegant basket—live clusters made of different varieties of roses in a range of pastel colors, supported by a subtle cascade of passion vine. The basket includes Ritz white roses, light pink Piaget, dark pink Prince Jardinier, silvery pink, Lavender Silverstone, and passion vine. ■

RESTAURANT DANIEL

RESTAURANT DANIEL

Restaurant DANIEL's neoclassical décor was brilliantly reinvented by designer Adam Tihany, who added delicate touches of contemporary flair. I love the fact that Daniel Boulud's soul is so clearly at ease in this new shell with its white palette, *frosted glass*, and clean-cut lines. Just like his cuisine, the décor now balances *tradition* and *modernity* in equal proportions.

In the alcove off the main dining room, the 18-foot-high coffered ceiling tops a monumental multitiered shelf. I am given free rein and regularly decorate it in a myriad of ways with plants, flowers, and objects. Here, the stunning Daum African sculpture collection inspired me to create a fantasy jungle inhabited by a wildly colored orange elephant and a purple rhinoceros, growing out of the plants. Around them I create a story winding along the various levels of the shelf, using color and light to drive the eye to the focal elements—the main animal characters.

In my African tableau, a sculpted antelope in steel and ebony jumps above golden

bushes of vanda orchids (opposite). I use the height of the installation to give the illusion of dimension—each tier of plants and flowers can appear to overlap one another, as though the viewer is looking at a natural landscape. I love the artistic freedom Daniel has accorded me over the years to express many different themes throughout the restaurant.

Tall and dramatic pale yellow eremurus stretch high in my imaginary jungle. I take advantage of the frosted light fixtures between a golden Daum glass lion and a purple hippopotamus, willing them to act as snowy clouds transfixed by spearlike Gymea lily leaves.

I like to soften the transition between stems and container. I stretch ribbons of Gymea leaves on top of the rectangular glass vase, and large philodendron leaves are placed underwater in the vases to provide a glimpse into

an aquatic world (above). My real cactus garden rounds up the tropical landscape while the two magnificent Daum cacti add a whimsical touch. Orange vanda orchids spring out of ceramic books on the lower ledge, next to Barker Bush.

THE SINATRA TREASURES

PICASSO   painter and sculptor in clay

Daniel Boulud

BRAISE DANIEL BOULUD

Daniel Boulud and   Daniel Boulud's
Dorie Greenspan   Café Boulud Cookbook

Cooking with DANIEL BOULUD

UD DANIEL'S DISH

CHEF DANIEL BOULUD

BRAISE DANIEL BOULUD

People use the word "organic" in so many different ways. I adjust and tinker until the overall look feels organic to me—as if there can be no other choice of elements and placement—a rightness of the whole that allows each element to be in its proper orbit.

My passion for Pablo Picasso's and Georges Braque's Cubist work infuses this scene. An homage to Daniel's work appears in the lower right corner in the form of his latest cookbooks, extending the horizontal lines of the book spines in a suffused light (opposite). Yellow arachnis orchids wrapped in Gymea leaves tower above a minimal flowering cactus garden. A bouquet of green kalanchoe adds to the tropical atmosphere.

The translucent Daum elephant towers over the scene, poking his head through the jungle brush, trumpeting his dominance.

In the world of courtly love, the time of Albrecht Dürer or the devilish Hieronymus Bosch, a dashing knight delivers a secret bouquet. Is it a peace offering? A statement of undying affection? Will his amorous and unusual gift win her love? Traditional concepts are discarded and a modern riff on a medieval theme takes shape in this unique arrangement.

Manolo Valdés's portraits add a mysterious and whimsical atmosphere to green spider mums surrounded by hanging amaranthus (opposite). They are wrapped in 'Moonlight' philodendron and burgundy calathea leaves (below). ▓

THE CASHIN–JOHNSON GUEST ROOM

In the apartment that interior designers Tom Cashin and Jay Johnson share, the walls hold a unique collection of photos and art chronicling their life during the high-flying Andy Warhol years. Decorative artifacts and works of art reflect their owners' eye and sense of humor, from the McDermott and McGough painting over the bed to the bright colors of the Billy Sullivan and Nan Goldin photographs.

I drew inspiration from "Joey Dressed for Wigstock," the Nan Goldin photograph of a seductive Joey Gabriel wearing a gargantuan headdress and a velvet burgundy costume, and decided to "dress" the lamps on either side of the bed, rather than upset the balance of the room by adding a more conventional flower arrangement.

I removed the paper shade, replaced it with a roll of chicken wire, and glued pink and crimson carnations in the hexagonal mesh to create my own interpretation of a playful floral coif (opposite). ■

THE VOLLBRACHT APARTMENT

THE VOLLBRACHT APARTMENT

I particularly admire artist and designer Michael Vollbracht's fashion acumen and sharp sense of style. Celebrated for his work with Bill Blass and Geoffrey Beene, in addition to his years as one of *The New Yorker*'s top illustrators, Mr. Vollbracht now concentrates on his artwork and collects unusual objects. His small ground-floor railroad apartment is a treasure trove of *exotic artifacts* and *salvaged pieces*, to which he adds personal touches. On the wall, one of his signature three-dimensional *collages* tells the tragic story of John F. Kennedy Jr.

Struck by the allegory of the soaring blackbird, I gathered

majestic feathers, a red tillandsia bromeliad, a wisteria vine, and croton leaves to build my own stark memorial to interrupted hope. On the side of the vase, an eighteenth-century shoe, part of Mr. Vollbracht's collection, adds an unexpected rococo detail (opposite). The half-moon container holds wheatgrass and underlines the tidal

renewal of nature. In my bouquets and arrangements I am not limited to flowers and plants. Objects, in this case feathers and an antique shoe, can achieve the same goal— to make one pause, touched by beauty and purpose.

A dry arrangement playing off the colors and tones of its surroundings can achieve as much as living plants. I painted a subtle forest with hekia branches and added screw-pine balls and a fan made of shelf mushroom (above). The opaque container plays the role of the tree trunk, the sturdy supporting actor.

When I was young and finally got to Paris, I spent many afternoons wandering the Louvre, captivated by the huge paintings by David and Delacroix, with their intricate detail and epic scope. My own style took me in an entirely modern direction, and I am never as happy as when I can create my own abstract art, with a touch of sci-fi and a shameless wink to styles past.

I see this half-moon vase as a long ship on which float flowers and grasses reminiscent of birds of paradise. An overarching wisteria vine extends the reach of my creation and protects the elegant green and white ensemble, which is inspired by the chic wallpaper and the plates displayed on the wall (opposite).

At the core of the arrangement, large king proteas—rarely seen in white—and anthuriums dominate green and white hosta leaves (above). Poppy pods burst toward the vine while long bear grass and dyplocyclos accompany the legs of the pedestal, crawling to the floor.

Above the fireplace, a genteel African ram standing on top of an antique file cabinet seems poised for a delicious run on the wheatgrass (opposite top). I planted beehive ginger plants to suggest a magical forest in the same color range as the Robert Motherwell lithograph Michael Vollbracht rescued from a pile of debris on the street. On the floor, large yellow croton plants add a touch of sun (opposite bottom).

Flowers tower over this real-life homage to Cézanne. Under the watchful eye of the African totem, a buffet table of tropical fruits (opposite) winks at the owner's other home in Florida. A bowl of *Allium schubertii* makes the link between flowers and plants. In the opaque ceramic vase, an explosion of blue statice expands the color palette and brings intensity to the table. In the clear vase, I mimic the shape of the totem and let its blue agapanthus nod to the powerful history of still-life painting and allegory.

There is a French expression I love, *lécher les vitrines*, which means "window-shopping" but translates literally to "licking the windows." Who can resist a stroll on the Faubourg Saint-Honoré in Paris, eating up the fabulous still-life window creations?

In the napping area, I studied the art on the walls and tried to absorb its essence, as in a stroll past familiar places. To develop the bouquets and arrangements and to enhance their surroundings, I wrapped the vases with birch bark for an organic look. Not wanting to detract from the displayed artifacts, I picked 'Orange Parrot' heliconia for the delicacy of their "fingers." At the base, croton leaves appear to grow out of the birch.

On the other end table, Michael's mask, seemingly out of *La divina commedia*, is surrounded by a symphony of pinks and reds (opposite). Gloriosa lilies, part stars and part magical hair, round out this tableau.

My constant challenge is to imagine people living and interacting with my imagined tableaux in their real-life world. No longer strangers behind the glass, they become a part of my whimsy.

Birch, tree trunks, sugarcanes, flower bulbs, or coconuts; there are myriad ways to bring nature at its most raw and pure into the home. I suggest a tropical forest in a guest room or design a vertical panorama along the wall of a simple bathroom (opposite). Cognac anthurium rest on rolls of galax leaves, while wisteria vine threatens to climb all the way to the sky. ■

163

THE FLEMING MUSIC ROOM

Our favorite diva just got home from singing in the matinée performance of *La Traviata* at the Metropolitan Opera. An hour ago the curtain fell and world-renowned soprano Renée Fleming took her bows to the standing ovation of a packed house. Her midnight blue gown rests on the piano bench, the opulent bouquet she received from an adoring fan now embellishes the Steinway. What better choice than a hundred red Baccara roses for an artist who brings passion to a different role every night? Taking my inspiration from the ethereal plumes sewn on the dress, I surrounded the immense bouquet with *Asparagus plumosus,* for its light and voluptuous feel. The silk ribbon wraps itself around the exuberant flowers, mimicking a Belle Epoque boa, and the philodendron leaf, folded in half, adds an haute couture touch. ■

THE CARLYLE HOTE

The Carlyle Hotel makes me dream about its *charmed past* with fancy parties and Gatsbyesque characters. This *Art Deco* splendor on Madison Avenue housed stars and dignitaries from around the world, as it continues to do today, and it is always an honor to devise flower arrangements for its celebrated rooms and suites. Most of them feature an expansive *view* over Central Park and the urban skyline.

The Empire Suite, a wood-paneled, three-bedroom duplex apartment on the 28th and 29th floors, was decorated by interior designer Thierry Despont, whose work I admire greatly. I chose flowers in the mauve palette, my favorite Roaring Twenties color. To fit seamlessly within his French and American Deco atmosphere, I construct two interior towers, one with purple gladioli, the other with purple and white gladioli, to mirror the city horizon across the verdant expanse of Central Park (opposite). A third bouquet combines purple with purple and white lisianthus.

Many pieces of furniture in the Empire Suite belonged to its prior owners before the apartment was sold to Rosewood Hotels. When objects fit perfectly in a space, it makes my job both easier and more difficult. Easier, as there is a rightness to the organization; harder, as the addition of flowers and plants must complement and extend this perfection.

The metal vase seems to grow as an extension of the 1940s Parisian console, the ideal vessel for classic white dahlias and hosta leaves (opposite). What more needs to be added?

Ochre, reds, and circular shapes embody the spirit of an intimate Art Deco salon. On the small table, viburnum branches meld their stringy stems to the warm hues. A red terra-cotta pot holds red vanda orchids with their crescent-shaped leaves, mimicking the movement of the armchairs and the table feet (below). At the bottom of the arrangement, baby tears unfurl a delicate green carpet.

The confluence of straight lines and verticality are immortalized in the vintage postcards and frames of these historic buildings (below). I wanted to acknowledge a dimension beyond the rectangles and squares that comprise this scene, so the roundness of the 'Estelle' roses and 'Blushing Bride' proteas supported by clarinervium leaves peek from their vase towers, with models of my favorite buildings below (opposite). What better place for an early morning breakfast?

Two different kinds of flowers tied together exist as separate statements and convey diverse emotions. 'Hot Ambiance' roses seem a wink to the past; 'Red Sox' calla lilies lend their futuristic shape to a timeless look. ■

THE EINBENDER RESIDENCE

THE EINBENDER RESIDENCE

Joan and Alvin Einbender gave free rein to their architect and friend Charles Gwathmey to create a 6,000-square-foot, 25-foot-high apartment within the *steel trussed volume* of a *former gymnasium*. Carved under the spirited Beaux Arts domes and roofs of the old police headquarters building on Manhattan's Lower East Side, this prodigious space with its *natural light* channeled through perfectly placed skylights reminds me of the Musée d'Orsay in Paris and serves as the perfect vessel for the owners' extraordinary art collection.

Every single object in the stunning Einbender residence is a design statement. And the smaller it is, the more it reverberates against the immensity and beauty of the space. On the long dining table designed by Gwathmey, waves of Alvar Aalto vases flow up and down, some transparent, allowing for my signature leaves, others an opaque white (opposite). There is no need for a tablecloth, but next to each plate I meld nature's elegance—an intricate knot made of a horsetail strand—with a simple black napkin. Mrs. Einbender's favorite colors and flowers, pink and white dahlias and purple tulips, evoke a sense of youth and femininity. Be it an event to benefit New York City Ballet or a beloved granddaughter's birthday lunch, a sense of serenity is palpable even though the party is about to start.

As soon as I met *Serene in Suspense,* a stunning Tom Shannon sculpture attached to the ceiling (opposite), I was struck by her completely relaxed pose. I saw her as a kind of modern Sleeping Beauty and immediately started to build in my mind a fantasy bed for her delicate frame so she could rest comfortably. Air currents allow the beautiful *Serene* to move, but the clever magnet hidden in her head continuously leads her back to true north. Flowers and plants' breaths constantly lead me to expand my creative limits, but they also represent my own true north.

Layers of wheatgrass and white gerbera daisies lie quietly beneath her, awaiting her repose.

When my eyes landed on this black ceramic vase in a Paris shop, I immediately pictured the green glass table, modeled after Joan Einbender's favorite Aalto vases, set on three bowling balls, and designed by Gwathmey (opposite). The vase's height and stature hold their own within the monumental volume, but its curves, the delicacy of the eucalyptus leaves, and their slightly smoky aroma bring femininity and lightness. A long fastened belt made of horsetails links the green of the leaves to the bluish tint of the table.

To reflect Donald Baechler's stunning world tapestry, I made my own floral globe out of blue hydrangea and 'Super Green' roses (below).

Stepping outside onto the exquisite terrace located off the kitchen, I am hit full force with the grandeur and elegance of this building, transporting me to the roof-tops of Paris or maybe Rome. From afar, bouquets of white dahlias, nigella pods, and 'Green Trick' dianthus surrounded by delicate clouds of *Asparagus plumosus* resemble miniature trees and cast long shadows over an elegant breakfast setting. For a small table, I've found that three similar arrangements—but of different heights and different volumes—often make more of an impact than one large bouquet (opposite). ◼

OLIVIER'S APARTMENT

OLIVIER'S APARTMENT

In my own home, I am always looking for new forms of *artistic* expression. From floral designer and creative director, I evolve again, this time letting my own taste, inspiration, and eye take the lead, as my apartment becomes a laboratory for new style ideas and experiments. I try to paint a *magical* landscape with artwork, collections, and even furniture I bring back from my *travels*. While I always strive to absorb and reflect my clients' tastes and personalities to enhance their environments, in my private world, I free my mind and engrave a more personal imprint.

A bookshelf is a blank canvas. It's an opportunity to tell a story, and in my case it's an opportunity to tell *my* story. I love how this shelf, like my world, is entirely unpredictable. Animals in bronze and mythic beasts, books, flowers, sculptures, and artifacts all brought home from different places I have visited are united by the leaves that frame my life and work.

For my own home, I love the grand gesture (or two), but I also revel in the small and intricate collection. At the top, Hawaiian dendrobium orchids bubble around an orchid photograph by Robert Mapplethorpe. Long horsetails with their bamboo identities lead the way down to an elephant found in Thailand.

Orange celosia with shelf mushrooms offer an intense pleated fabric picking up the earth tone of the vase. On the right, orange *Asclepias tuberosa* with philodendron leaves line an imaginary garden where my nephews play.

Brigitte Bardot, Apple of My Eye, Star of My Southern Youth!

Only the color red and only a significant vase can stand up to her alluring gaze (opposite). This majestic lava stone urn made by my friend Alain Vagh holds dashing sunflowers (below), a wink to my native Provence. Monumental philodendron leaves serve as ruffle, and strands of bear grass reflect the actress's blond mane, while two hornet's nests might make one think of the star's famous décolletage.

Pour Olivier
with all my love
Brigitte Bardot

ISABELLE HUPPERT

This morning the news fell. The King of Pop is dead. In my music room, I celebrate his life with the help of my flower friends. White phalaenopsis orchids and their artificial counterparts, metal phalaenopsis orchids (above right), laid on top of a 1970s mirrored coffee table (opposite), turn into an improvised tribute. His white gloves and metallic costumes will stay with me, as will his unique melodies and dance moves. Mini copies of the Statue of Liberty resembling white angels (above left) inhabit this fantasy garden.

On the right side, my own sculpture made of fiber-optic filament cables rounds out this tableau.

199

Hanging behind my dining table, Alexander Vethers's black-and-white photograph of Neptune in the Tuileries garden of Paris (below) reminds me of the long walks I took there a few months after I moved to Paris, and the pleasure I always garnered watching the crowds move along the Place de la Concorde. My fall arrangement mirrors the antique stone cornucopia. A festival of autumn colors, it contains orange dahlias, red amaranthus, branches bearing quince fruits, green Santini chrysanthemums, shelf mushrooms, red chrysanthemums, and acorns (opposite).

In the bedroom, sensuality reigns and finds its expression through three arrangements of dark and mysterious flowers. This choice of flowers also pays homage to the beauty and purity of a pair of black-and-white nude photographs by Karl Lagerfeld hanging on the wall beside my bed.

In these multiple arrangements made of black calla lilies and chocolate cosmos wrapped simply with dark croton leaves (below left and right), I play with height and the subtle differences in hues and textures. The extreme contrast between the transparent square glass vases and the velvety darkness of the petals is something I particularly relish (opposite).

Now that you have visited my home and discovered my own personal landscape, let's go "backstage" so you can learn how to create your own arrangements. We will explore which tools can be most helpful and how simple techniques can yield gorgeous results. ∎

PART II

RECIPES

The easy techniques that you will find in the following pages will help you embellish your home and set the perfect mood for any occasion. Don't be intimidated. Your family and guests will be impressed and uplifted by your artistic sense and style. I will even share with you my styling tips and finishing touches, in particular my signature leaf-wrapping methods. Take my recommendations as starting points and unleash your passion for nature.

Some of these arrangements showcase seasonal elements, cut flowers, branches, leaves and plants, dried and preserved items. Substitute one plant for another and one color for its opposite. Let your creativity guide you.

Once you have mastered an arrangement, challenge yourself to make a complementary one, varying size, color, and textures. As you saw in the previous section (see page 46 top, Kennedy, dining table), I placed five compositions on the breakfast table, including four different bouquets and one dry tableau on a rattan tray. On page 83, I covered my friend Freddie Leiba's dining room table with an exuberant array of exotic flowers, plants, candles, and fruit arrangements, creating the feel of a tropical jungle. Feel free to use the elements around you to make the composition reflect your personal touch. Pedestals for sculptures can become supports for plants or even bouquets, as you can see in the home of Jack Anderson (page 101). Frame a favorite painting with two identical arrangements or topiaries as I did at the Carroll home (pages 121–122). Dead branches or even bonsai can be recycled into a fantastic forest as on Jean-Claude Huon's Oriental console (page 33 left).

Let's elevate our mood and make floral art together.

RECIPES

Rose Pavé

The classic, hand-tied bouquet of the past has been replaced by this soft rose pillow, a square composition I connect to modern shapes and styles. On your coffee table, place several such arrangements, varying colors, size, and varieties of flowers, to create a welcoming burst of cheerfulness.

MATERIALS

1 square clear glass vase about 6 inches long, 6 inches wide,
*   and 4 inches high*
1 aspidistra leaf, cut to fit edges of vase
16 red roses, medium size
2 bricks of floral foam, soaked
Knife to cut the leaf, the stems, and the floral foam
Scissors to trim the leaf

Notes: For roses you can substitute any other round-headed flower such as pincushion flowers and orchids. Thanks to its small size, the pavé can also be displayed in a bookshelf. As on page 58 top (Venokur), several pincushion pavés are tucked among plates and glassware.

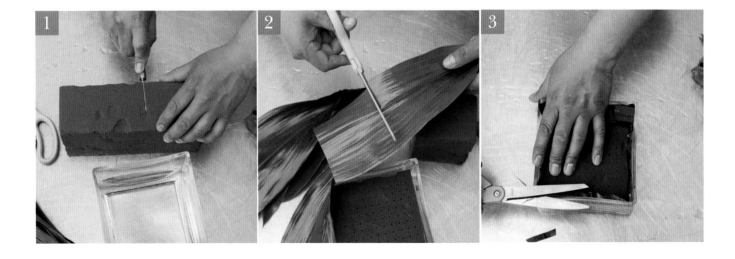

UPKEEP: Fill the container almost to the rim with cold water mixed with flower food. Add fresh water every other day and remove wilted petals. This arrangement should last 1 week.

COMPOSITION

1 Trim the floral foam to fit snugly into the square vase.

2 Wrap the four sides of the square-shaped floral foam with the trimmed aspidistra leaf, shiny side out.

3 Trim flush to the floral foam. Place the wrapped floral foam into the container.

4 Cut the rose stems, leaving a pointy 2-inch stem. Remove broken or wilted petals. Plant the roses in the floral foam in 4 rows of 4 flowers, mixing large and small flowerheads.

Bathing Calla Lilies

Bringing to mind a young lady reclining in her vaporous bath, the flowers lazily rest their stems in a pose reminiscent of 1930s glamour. The erotic calla lily continues to inspire artists and photographers. Let it bring a touch of sensuality to your home.

Notes: This surprisingly stylish arrangement can decorate a bookshelf, where it will attract the eye with its elegant movement; see page 58 (Venokur). A larger variation of this bouquet, this time featured as a stunning centerpiece, is showcased on page 77 (Grey).

MATERIALS

1 clear glass rectangular vase, about 16 inches long, 4 inches wide, and 4 inches high
2 aspidistra leaves, shined
20 mango-colored calla lilies, at least 20 inches long, divided into 2 bunches of 10 stems each

Green raffia to secure
Measuring tape
Knife to cut the stems
Scissors to trim leaves

1 Shape each aspidistra leaf into a rectangle of about 6 by 4 inches by cutting off the tip and stem with the scissors.

2 Gently rub your hand a few times over each calla lily stem. Your palm's warmth will allow you to bend the flexible stem slightly. Once shaped, place 10 stems in your hand, one at a time, checking that each flower head is lined up to the previous one.

3 Make sure that the stems are long enough to rest against one end of the vase while the flowers lay their heads on the other side. Wrap 1 rectangular piece of aspidistra leaf around the end of the stems. Tie the bunch with raffia, going around several times to make sure the stems stay in place, and cut the extra string. Cut the extra stems sticking out, flush to wrap. Repeat the same procedure for the second bunch, making sure that both are similar in size.

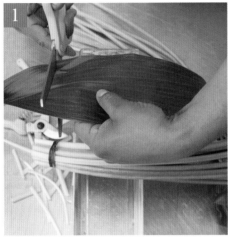  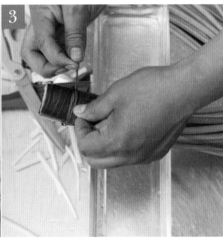

4 Lay the first bunch into the vase by pushing the stem tips against the short inside edge and by resting the necks of the calla lilies on the opposite edge with the flowers facing up. Place the second bunch in the vase across from the first.

5 Cut two 4-inch pieces from the leftover stems to fit snugly within the width of the vase. These cylinders will hold the flowers down in the vase. Place 1 cylinder over the neck of each bunch, pushing gently down until flush with the rim of the vase.

UPKEEP: Fill the vase halfway with cold water mixed with flower food. Add fresh water daily and change water every 2 days. Remove any wilted petals. This arrangement should last 1 week.

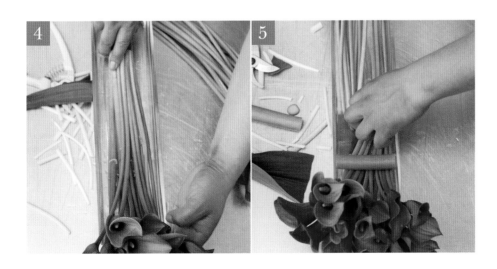

White Orchid Cascade

For Christina Onassis's lavish wedding to Thierry Roussel at Maxim's in Paris, the Belle Epoque room was bursting with cascading white orchids. At the top of the decorative pillars, hundreds of precious phalaenopsis rippled down, echoing the bride's gorgeous bouquet. Waves of sumptuous abundance emanated from this luxurious and festive arrangement.

Notes: Phalaenopsis come in many colors, such as pink, lavender, and yellow. Match the color of the vase to that of the flower for a more stunning effect. The more stylish the vase, the more elegant the ensemble will be.

COMPOSITION

1 Fill the bottom of the vase with a slightly bunched cellophane sheet to keep the bouquet elevated. Fill 3/4 of the vase with water for stability. Fan out 3 stems of phalaenopsis in your hand, as you would playing cards. If there is a flower bud at the tip of a stem, extend the stem beyond the length of the others. Tie the 3 stems together with green tape. Repeat

twice, leaving the extra phalaenopsis stems to fill in holes at the end.

2 Take the first bunch and place 4 or 5 geranium leaves around base of the first flowers. Add the second bunch and more geranium leaves. And the third.

3 Tie the ensemble with green tape, keeping stems and geranium leaves

close together. Place the bouquet delicately in the vase. Spread out the stems to expand the reach.

4 Add the 3 extra phalaenopsis stems to fill any holes.

5 To ease the visual transition between the vase and orchid stems, insert a philodendron stem in the

MATERIALS

1 tall white glass vase, about 20 inches tall and 8
  inches in diameter
1 large sheet clear cellophane to fill the vase
12 white phalaenopsis stems with about 10 flower
  heads each, stems 25 to 30 inches long
1 bunch geranium leaves
3 philodendron leaves
1 bunch lily grass
Natural color wire-bound raffia
Waterproof green tape
Pruners to cut the wire-bound raffia

vase at the back of the cascading phalaenopses. Push the body of the leaf, wrapping it against the outside neck of the vase, and keep in place with raffia. Repeat with the second leaf. Place the stem of the third leaf in between first 2, roll the tip of the leaf into the vase, and tuck its sides under the 2 neighboring leaves.

6 Roll 1/2 bunch of lily grass around your fingers, as you would a strand of hair to make a curl. Tie lily grass with raffia at the base and tip. Place the base of the lily grass strand in the vase between the philodendron leaves and tuck the tips toward the front of the vase between orchid heads, creating an organic bridge between the philodendron leaf and

the phalaenopsis flowers. Attach the tucked tip with raffia to an orchid stem to secure its position. Repeat a second time.

UPKEEP: Fill the vase with water and flower food every 2 to 3 days. Remove wilted flowers. This bouquet should last a week to 10 days.

Stylized Orchid Garden

As you build the orchid's new habitat, imagine yourself in a tropical forest, brushing against the smooth bamboos, the soft moss, and the silky orchid flowers. Let the inherent beauty of the orchid touch you and whisper whiffs of exotic lands.

MATERIALS

1 bowl, 8 inches in diameter and 4 inches deep
½ bag of stones, enough to layer the bottom of the bowl, to drain excess water
1 orchid plant, 20 to 30 inches tall
3 peperomias or similar small plants requiring little water
⅓ of a moss tray
3 white decorative crystals
2 bamboo sticks, one 20 to 30 inches tall, depending on length of orchid, and one 10 inches tall
Natural wire-bound raffia to secure
Leaf shine
Pruning shears to cut wire-bound raffia

Notes: As you choose the small ornamental plants to accompany the orchid, make sure to select varieties that need as little water as the orchid. This composition works for every variety of orchid plant—just pick your favorite one. Once you have mastered a single-stem orchid garden, try larger arrangements showcasing multiple orchids.

1 Place the stones in the bowl. Remove the orchid from its plastic pot and transfer the plant into the bowl.

2 Transfer the small green plants and their surrounding soil into the bowl, around the orchid.

3 Place the moss on top of the soil and push it snugly inside the bowl around the plants.

4 Remove the plastic garden stake holding the orchid stem up. Replace it with a bamboo pole. Tie the stem

to the bamboo with the wire-bound raffia. Trim the top of the bamboo at a pleasing height. Plant a second piece of bamboo at the edge of the bowl, leaning it toward the vertical bamboo, and tie them together for added visual effect.

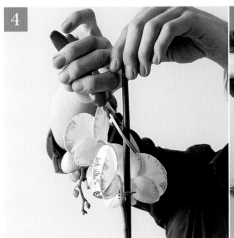 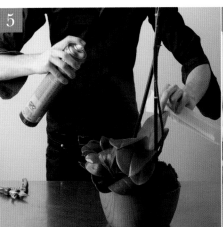 

5 Spray the leaves with shine and remove excess with a paper towel.

6 Display crystals at base of the arrangement.

UPKEEP: Add a little water to the bowl every 3 days. Keep the orchid away from drafts. The flowers should last 1 month. Cut the dead flowers. The plant may flower several times a year.

Autumn Folly

One of the greatest thrills of living on the East Coast is the ability to leave the cities and drive north to admire the fiery fall foliage with its luscious and intense colors. With this hand-tied bouquet, you can recapture autumn's burning romance in your home.

Notes: An autumn arrangement includes reds, oranges, and yellows and seasonal fruits and vegetables, such as plums and grapes. I always mix textures and add green leaves to round out a seasonal feel.

COMPOSITION

1 Remove the thorns and leaves of the rose stems with a knife, leaving the 2 top leaves. Remove the lower leaves of the gloriosa stems. Remove lower leaves from the small magnolia branches, leaving only foliage at the tip. Apply spray shine to the rose hips. Wrap 2 wires around the dried white husk of the corn, next to the kernels. Twist them to create a wire stem about 4 inches long.

2 Take a rose in your hand, holding it vertically. Add 6 more, one by one, turning the bunch slightly as you add each one. Add 4 rose hip stems, keeping them in a bunch.

3 Add 3 ears of baby corn on the opposite side of the berries. Add 3 green leaves under the corn, tucking their tips into your hand. Add more roses around the corn. Add the calla lilies in a cluster between the roses and the corn. Add more roses and berries.

MATERIALS

6 dried ears of red baby corn
   with white husks
25 orange roses
5 gloriosa lily stems
5 small magnolia branches
1 bunch of rose hips
2 aspidistra leaves
15 orange calla lilies
1 bunch of dyed red eucalyptus
12 thin floral wires for the corn
Waterproof green tape
Spray shine for the rose hips
Raffia or several strands of lily grass

Knife to cut stems and
   remove thorns
Pruning shears to cut
   branches and wire
Scissors to trim the dried
   cornhusk

4 Add the gloriosa and the magnolia leaves, continuously turning the bouquet in your hand. If the bouquet is getting too big for your hands, tie it with the green tape as you go along. Add the eucalyptus to one side, so that it hangs over the vase. Tie the finished bouquet with green tape. Cut off the stems at an angle to fit the vase.

5 Wrap the stems with the aspidistra leaves and hold them in place with a ribbon of lily grass or raffia.

6 Place the bouquet in the vase filled with water mixed with flower food. Trim the dried white husk of corn with scissors.

UPKEEP: Change the water every other day, adding flower food. Trim the stems of the arrangement for better hydration. This bouquet should last 1 week.

Eastern Oak Branches

Don't be afraid to bring tall branches into your home. Place this airy composition on the floor or on a low table. You will enjoy the peacefulness of its graceful lines.

MATERIALS

1 cylinder glass vase, 18 inches high and
  6 inches in diameter
3 pieces of birch bark, enough to line the vase
5 oak branches with acorn, 4 feet long
5 curly willow branches, 6 feet long
1 bunch sansevieria leaves
3 bricks of floral foam, soaked
Natural raffia to secure
Scissors to cut raffia
Pruning shears to cut branches

Notes: When displaying several types of branches in the same composition, I make certain that one variety does not overwhelm the other with its volume of foliage, and I keep them in separate corners of the container.

1 Roll the pieces of bark around the vase to encircle it completely. Tie with raffia near the bottom and the top. Make sure the bark covers the vase entirely.

2 Insert the floral foam at the bottom of the vase, filling up to ⅔ of the

vase. Measure the branches against the vase to see how much of the branches need to be cut off. See the tip on how to cut branches on page 237.

3 Plant the oak branches into the floral foam on one side of the vase,

using ½ of the space. Make sure that the branches all curve in the same direction, toward the center, to create the illusion of movement.

4 On the other side of the vase, plant the curly willow. To rein in the strands, twist the tips together.

5 Plant a sansevieria stem into the floral foam and bring the tip around the outside of the vase. Secure the tip with raffia tied around the neck of the vase.

6 Repeat with the rest of the leaves, sticking them in the floral foam a few

inches farther to the left from the previous one. Trim any loose strands and leaves from the bottom of the branches for a clean look.

UPKEEP: Fill the vase with water mixed with floral food. Add water

every other day and remove wilted leaves. This arrangement should last 2 weeks, except for the decorative sansevieria leaves, which you can replace when wilted.

Wheatgrass and Dahlia Meadow

Imagine a spring picnic on this fantasy meadow right in your home. Whether on your kitchen table or on the floor of your living room, this whimsical beauty is sure to delight children of all ages.

MATERIALS

*Clear rectangular Plexiglas container, 30 inches long,
  20 inches wide, and 3 inches high
2½ wheatgrass flats
50 pompon dahlias
5 bricks floral foam, soaked
Knife to cut the wheatgrass and stems
Measuring tape
Scissors to trim the wheatgrass*

Notes: By choosing flower heads of the same size, I create a symmetrical ensemble, pleasing to the eye. Dahlias come in many colors; select one that will fit your décor best.

1 Measure the length of the rectangular container and mentally divide it into 3 equally sized areas, 10 inches long by 20 inches wide. Two will be filled with the wheatgrass, and the middle area with the flowers. Cut the wheatgrass with a knife to fit within 2 of these areas.

2 Place the grass snugly in the container, framing the rectangle for the flowers. Connect both grass rectangles with 2 thin grass strips running along the sides of the container.

3 Fill the empty center rectangle with floral foam bricks. The floral foam should reach 1 inch under the wheatgrass tops.

4 With the knife, cut the flower stems at an angle, leaving 3-inch stems, and stick the flower heads into the flower foam, starting at one of the corners. Keep the flowers in

rows. Feel free to add more flowers to keep the center tighter.

5 Trim the wheatgrass blade tops evenly with your scissors for a cleaner look.

UPKEEP: Spray the wheatgrass with water, and sparingly water the dahlias daily. This arrangement should last 1 week.

Romantic White Rose Orb

Versailles was known the world over for its rose gardens. Re-create Marie-Antoinette's delightful artistry with this sweet and dreamy rose bubble. Three different varieties of white roses adorn this composition for a soft *camaïeu* effect, sure to seduce the romantic hearts in your household.

Notes: Let your creativity dictate whether to use roses, orchids, pincushions, dahlias, or any other flower with a round head. Choose the colors, tones, or textures that work best in your interior. You can also cut the floral-foam sphere in half, for a more economical arrangement. On page 8 (Howard), 3 different spheres coexist artfully on a coffee table. On page 181 (Einbender), a large green and blue sphere mimics our beautiful planet Earth.

COMPOSITION

1 Cut the stems of the roses to 2 inches for the larger variety and 3 inches for the smaller one. Remove falling petals.

2 Plant the largest flower first at the top of the sphere and keep the others level, always inserting each stem toward the center of the sphere.

3 Keep the flower heads in clusters of the same variety and close together to hide the floral foam. You can leave the bottom part empty so that the sphere will stand easily on a flat surface.

MATERIALS

One 8-inch diameter floral-foam sphere, soaked
50 white roses, about ⅓ each of the 'Vendela', 'Escimo',
  and Majolica varieties
Knife to cut the stems

4 Display on a stand, a plate, or directly on the table, but protect the furniture from the water that can flow from the soaked floral foam.

UPKEEP: This arrangement will last 5 days or even longer if you spray it daily with water.

Twin Hydrangea Vessels

The best hosts know how to create fascinating connections between guests at their dinner parties. These vessels, organically coupled to each other with strands of delicate ivy, weave nature and artistry together, promoting pleasant relationships around the table.

Notes: When placing the finished arrangements on the table, shift one vase in front of the other. I have deliberately chosen a different number of candles of different heights per vase and placed them in asymmetrical positions for a more visually interesting look. Depending on the size of your table, feel free to multiply the number of vases and connect them with ivy. Do not let candles burn too close to the flowers. See page 23 (Huon), where a similar arrangement welcomes visitors in the foyer.

MATERIALS

*2 half-moon–shaped vases, 12 inches long,
   3 inches wide, and 7 inches high*
*8 white hydrangeas, medium to large heads,
   4 per vase*
3 to 4 ivy strands
3 tall white candles
*12 pieces of thin floral wire, cut to 6 inches,
   to secure candles in the floral foam*
*3 six-inch waterproof green tape ribbons,
   one for each candle*
4 bricks floral foam, soaked, 2 for each vase
Pruning shears to cut wire
Scissors to cut green tape

1 Fill the vase with cut-to-fit floral foam, flush to the surface.

2 Split the hydrangea heads into 3 or 4 florets each, leaving a 2- to 3-inch stem. Stick the flowers in the floral foam along one edge first, letting them hang elegantly over the side of the vase.

3 Repeat this process on the other side. Prepare the second vase in the same manner.

4 Place both vases on the table, leaving a space in between. Remove leaves at the bottom of the ivy branch and plant it into the farthest corner of the first vase. Guide the branch toward the front of the vase and secure

it under the bottom of the second vase. Add a second stem and repeat. Place a third stem in the second vase and bring it over the flowers, slide the end into the vase.

5 Place 4 wire sticks around the base of each candle and tie them securely to the candle with green tape.

6 Delicately plant 2 candles into the first arrangement through the foam be-tween flower heads, and place the last candle into the second arrangement.

UPKEEP: Add water mixed with flower food every other day. This arrangement should last 1 week to 10 days.

Fall Harvest Centerpiece

Once a year, fall fruits and flowers can harmoniously set the stage for your Thanksgiving feast. Grateful for the season's bounty, your delectable centerpiece celebrates the harvest.

MATERIALS

1 clear glass bowl, 8 inches in diameter and 4 inches deep
6 aspidistra leaves, 3 to line the bowl and 3 in the arrangement
3 dozen fall-color roses, such as 'Coffee Break', 'Voodoo', and 'Black Magic'
1 bunch of rose hips

10 four-inch-long bamboo sticks, ¼ inch thick
3 hazel leaves
5 or 6 plums
1 large bunch of red grapes
1½ bricks of floral foam, soaked

COMPOSITION

1 Place the floral foam in the container. Shape it as seen in the photo (a topless pyramid with slightly rounded edges). Tape the floral foam to the plate with the two 12-inch strips, creating a cross. Secure the cross with the third piece of tape wrapped around the edge of the plate.

2 Cut the stems of the aspidistra leaves to 2 inches in length. Fold the cut pieces of stem in two, creating a hairpin, and set aside. Stick the stem of the first aspidistra leaf into the floral foam near the edge of the bowl and wrap it along the side. Thrust the pointy stem of the second leaf through the tip of the first one and into the floral foam. Continue wrapping the bowl until totally lined. To fasten the last tip to the bowl, use the hairpin-shaped piece of the aspidistra stem previously set aside and stick into the tip and leaves, through to the floral foam.

3 Roll an aspidistra leaf on itself, folding the tip back. Make sure to keep the shiny side of the leaf outside. Use the stem to pierce through both

*Notes: If you own a favorite opaque bowl you won't need to line it
with leaves. Clustering the various autumnal colors and elements
in this arrangement creates a beautiful palette.*

*3 pieces of waterproof green tape, two 12 inches in length
    and one long enough to go around the edge of the plate
Scissors to cut the tape
Knife to cut the roses
Pruning shears to cut the bamboo sticks and branches*

tip and leaf. Pull the stem through
and stick into the center of the arrangement. Repeat twice. Prepare the
rest of the elements. Cut off the stems
of the roses and rose hips, leaving a
2-inch pointy stem at an angle. Mount
each plum on a 4-inch bamboo stick.

4 Stick the yellow roses in a cluster next
to the top leaves and all the way down to
the edge of the bowl. Plant a row of rose
hips alongside the yellow roses, and then
a cluster of orange roses.

5 Place several bamboo sticks in the
floral foam and hang the grapes
around them. Use the hazel leaves
planted in a row to separate flower
clusters and fruits.

6 Plant the plums, more rose hips,
more leaves and red roses, and continue to fill in clusters.

UPKEEP: Add water every other day.
Remove wilted petals and replace rot-
ting fruit. This arrangement should
last 1 week.

Fantasy Camellia Tree

A magical camellia tree has sprouted in your home.
The camellia leaves now bloom out of a fluorescent trunk—
a fantastic statement. Become a wizard and expand the
limits of your reality.

MATERIALS

*1 tall, square clear vase 18 inches tall and
   6 inches wide*
4 large camellia branches
2 philodendron leaves
Water gel crystals
*Florist color powder such as Design Master A-36
   Yellow/Yellow or food coloring*
*1 stick, about 24 inches in length, to stir the color
   in the gelled water*
Green raffia to secure
Pruning shears to cut branches
Scissors to cut raffia

*Notes: You can substitute any other seasonal
branch for the camellia. Play with the colors of
your choice. Children around the house will enjoy
transforming the water into gel crystals, then
dyeing it a fantastic color.*

1 Fill half the vase with water. Add the required water gel crystals. The gelling process will raise the water level, as will the branches. Stir and let sit for at least 3 hours or even overnight until completely gelled.

2 Add a teaspoon (or more if necessary) of color powder and mix well with the long stick.

3 Measure the camellia branches against the vase to see how much

of the branches needs to be cut off. (See the tip on how to cut branches on page 239.)

4 Place the cut branches in the vase. Trim all bottom leaves and loose

strands. You want a clean set of branches before the top leafy part.

5 Insert the stem of the philodendron leaf into the neck of the vase and wrap its body around the outside of the neck. Secure with the green

raffia. Repeat the same process with the second leaf to finish enveloping the neck of the vase.

UPKEEP: This arrangement will last 5 days in the colored gel water and 2 weeks in fresh water.

229

Orange Wheat Field

There is a point in late summer when wheat fields become so golden they take on a brilliant orange tint. At dawn or at sunset, the fields seem ablaze. Bring this moment into your home and let the sun ignite your imagination.

Notes: As the dried stems of wheat can be brittle, handle them with care. Remove shedding pieces of stem by pulling them off with your hands. This arrangement is shown in a country home on page 29 (Huon). It can also be displayed in an urban setting, greeting visitors in your foyer, or be used to decorate your hearth.

COMPOSITION

1 Staple the coconut husk along the sides of the box to cover it. String the natural raffia twice around the box near the bottom, then around the top.

2 Fill the box snugly with dry foam.

3 Take a small bunch of wheat in your hand, leveling the heads. Cut off the bottom ends to equalize the height of the stems. Plant the bunch into the foam, starting at one corner of the box. Continue this process until the box is full, making sure all the heads are at the same level.

1 rectangular wooden flat, 18 inches long, 7 ½ inches wide, and 5 inches high
1 roll coconut husk, to line the outside of the container
250 long wheat stalks, dried and dyed orange (5 bunches of 50)
12 bamboo sticks: four 14-inch sticks for vertical use in corners, cut to reach slightly higher than half the height of the wheat; two 20-inch sticks cut to reach slightly longer than the length of the box
Two 8-inch sticks cut to reach slightly farther than the width of the box
Industrial staple gun to staple the coconut bark to the wooden container
Natural raffia for added style
3 floral foam bricks, do not soak
Wire-bound raffia to tie the bamboo sticks together
Pruning shears to cut bamboo sticks and wire

4 To hold the wheat together, build a bamboo gate: plant the 4 longest bamboo sticks at each corner of the box. Place a long stick horizontally, at a 90-degree angle, to close the gate. Twist-tie the wire raffia around the bamboo, make a knot, and cut off excess strands. Repeat this process on the other 3 sides.

5 Trim the wheat silk tops with scissors for a clean look.

UPKEEP. This arrangement will last 1 year. To remove dust, use a blow dryer.

231

Crimson Dream Lampshade

How can flowers ignite our passions? Bring them into the bedroom and onto our lampshades to celebrate Valentine's Day. Have them set the mood for a romantic evening as the shiny light will be gently filtered through the petals and glow with dreamy crimson beams.

MATERIALS

2 inexpensive small lampshades, about 12 inches tall by 8 inches in diameter
100 carnations, medium size, any color
Chicken wire, 2 pieces 3 feet by 3 feet

Wire
Knife to cut stems
Pruning shears to cut wire
Floral glue

COMPOSITION

1 Delicately remove the fabric from the lampshades. Replace the fabric with chicken wire and secure it with regular wire at the top and bottom.

2 Cut the stems completely off.

3 Spread floral glue on the base of each flower and place them one by one into the mesh.

Notes: This is a labor of love, as you will have to build the lamp-shade and then patiently pluck 50 flowers, all for an effect that will last only 24 hours. My friends decided to wear them first as fanciful hats to a Valentine's Day party before reattaching them to their nightstand lamps! (See pages 146 and 147, Cashin-Johnson.)

4 Continue until the chicken wire is completely covered. Let dry for at least an hour.

UPKEEP: Spray with water. The flowers will start wilting after a day.

PART III
GENERAL TIPS

Fresh flowers, plants, leaves, and branches depend on our nurturing skills to maximize their life span. Luckily there are sohme things we can do to help these wonderful beings thrive in our homes. I am delighted to share these with you and have also listed the necessary tools and containers and a few of my favorite suppliers.

SEASONAL ELEMENTS

I love to enhance homes with seasonal arrangements. They honor and celebrate nature's bounty and remind us of the yearly cycle of harvest and festivals. We get back in touch with what is growing in the fields, forests, and orchards. I pepper my arrangements with seasonal fruits and vegetables that can be found at your local farmer's markets. Most flower shops and nurseries also carry seasonal varieties; just ask! And keep in mind that flowers in season are sold at their lowest price.

When purchasing fresh elements for your bouquets and centerpieces, look for strong stems with fresh leaves and flower heads that have not yet fully bloomed. Look for fresh, unblemished produce. Choose seasonal fruit, not fully ripened, with a tough skin that will last if pierced with a bamboo stick you might use to secure it in an arrangement. Avoid juicy and delicate fruits and berries. Keep extra fruits and vegetables in your fridge to replace wilted ones. I often use fruits and vegetables in centerpieces for dinner parties. Artfully mixed with floral elements, they will help set the mood for a lavish feast.

As with produce, many floral ingredients are now available year-round, as they are imported from around the world. Popular flowers such as roses, tulips, and orchids

235

are bred to take on seasonal colors and should be included in your bouquets. My suggested seasonal list will therefore include not only authentic seasonal items, but also year-round favorites that I believe add to the seasonal feel of an arrangement.

Suggested fall elements

- Your color palette should include: deep reds, fiery oranges, and sunny yellows. Flowers: dahlias; orange amaryllis and tulips; rudbeckia; 'Charlie Brown' cymbidium orchids; marigolds; orange, yellow, and burgundy calla lilies.
- Branches: magnolia, pear, maple, rose hips, wild huckleberries, olive branches.
- Leaves: red ti leaves, hazel, photinia.
- Fillers: rose hips, hypericum berries, asclepias, leucadendron.
- Fruit and vegetables: small apples, plums, grapes, baby pears, persimmons, pomegranates, walnuts and chestnuts, ornamental cabbage, cauliflower, garlic heads, mushrooms, pumpkins and squash, Indian corn.

On page 226 you will learn how to make a fall harvest centerpiece, and on page 216 an autumn-folly hand-tied bouquet.

Suggested winter elements

- Your color palette should include: cool whites, icy blues, or bright colors.
- Flowers: ranunculus, hellebores, red or white tulips, anemones, white orchids.
- Branches: flowering quince, evergreens, pussy willow.
- Leaves: tropical leaves, such as monstera or aspidistra.
- Fillers: cedar, wax flowers.
- Fruit and vegetables: citrus fruits, tropical fruits, dried fruits, baby pineapples, Brussels sprouts, fennel, baby parsnips and turnips, broccoli florets.

Suggested spring elements

- Your color palette should include: tender greens and pastels.
- Flowers: flowering bulbs such as tulips and the fragrant hyacinths, the eremurus or foxtail lily, muscari, fritillaria, crocus, daffodils, peonies, and the sweet pea. Lily of the valley is my favorite spring flower and, as we do in

France on May 1, I always offer my friends a fresh bouquet of them to mark the passing of winter.

- Branches: cherry blossom, dogwood, forsythia, lilac, azaleas, viburnum, blueberries, rhododendron, Scotch broom.
- Leaves: camellia, bay leaves.
- Fillers: lady's mantle, fresh mint, scented geraniums.
- Fruits and vegetables: nectarines, prunes, lemons, artichokes, baby beets with leaves, baby white turnips, baby carrots, garlic sprouts, French string beans in a cluster, mushrooms, and sweet peppers.

Suggested summer elements

- Your color palette should include: yellows, white, blue, bright pinks.
- Flowers: blue delphiniums, gladioli, irises, sunflowers, hydrangeas, astilbes.
- Branches: crab apple, plum, smoke bush.
- Leaves: hostas, scented geraniums, philodendron.
- Fillers: scabiosa, basil, rosemary.
- Fruit and vegetables: yellow plums, nectarines, apricots, giant strawberries, red currants, pink radishes, olives, baby purple and/or white eggplants, scallions, yellow squash.

PREPARATION AND CARE
Cut Flowers

Well-cared-for flowers should last about a week. Always remove lower leaves and thorns with your knife and cut stems at an angle before placing in the vase for maximum hydration. Add flower food to the clean water. Every other day, remove wilted petals and change the water. Adding warm water will speed the opening of the flowers; cold water will slow down the process. Just top off the container with water mixed with flower food if it is too heavy or includes floral foam. If spraying with water, make sure to take the arrangement to the kitchen and let it dry there, to avoid water stains on your furniture.

Some cut flowers require just a few inches of water in the vase, for example, spring flowers such as calla lilies. For bulb flowers such as tulips and hyacinths, the stems will remain stronger with less water. (See on pages 104 and 105, Anderson white tulips on fireplace.) Add only a small quantity of water to the vase for these flowers.

Fillers

This term describes small-flowered stems. They are typically used by florists to enlarge a bouquet with less expensive items. To me, fillers are just as beautiful as any other flower, adding color or texture. I will make a bouquet just with gypsophila; the array of small white flowers reminds me of a cloud. On page 24 (Huon, living room table) the smaller bouquet is made solely with asclepias. On page 170 (Carlyle, living room table) I composed a bouquet of baby tears. Fillers have life spans similar to larger flowers and require the same care.

Leafy or Flowering Branches

Cutting fresh branches requires strength and therefore can be difficult. Make sure to measure the exact length needed for the container and ask the florist to cut them to the desired height. If you decide to cut them yourself, patiently incise around the branch at the desired length with pruning shears. Incise deeper and deeper into the wood, going around as you cut. Once you are halfway through the wood, place the branch on a flat surface with the incised piece flush with the table and the extra end toward you. Snap off the extra end by pushing down on it with your body weight.

Cut the ends at an angle with the pruners and incise again, splitting in two for maximum hydration. Remove lower leaves and loose strands for a cleaner look.

Leafy branches can last 2 weeks if properly hydrated, and flowering branches about a week before the blossoms start to wilt. Every other day remove wilted blossoms and leaves and change the water (or add water if the container is too heavy to move). Add flower food with clear water.

Feel free to recycle your branches into new arrangements by cutting off any remaining flowers or leaves. Branches such as curly willow are decorative even without leaves.

Orchid Plants

Choose plants with at least 3 or 4 flowers and several buds as well as healthy-looking long, meaty, dark green leaves at the base. Make sure to place the plant in the most humid corner of your home, away from drafts and bright lights. Dry heat coming from the radiators can be harmful.

Add a little water to the plant every three days. After the flower dies, cut it at the knot. The plant can flower again every year.

Leaves

I often finish a composition with a tropical leaf, which has become one of my signature touches. These beautiful ornaments have a flexible body, which allows me to bend, roll, fold, and mold them. Depending on the arrangement and the role I want the leaf to play, I work with different sizes, colors, shapes, as well as finishes, shiny or matte. For a shiny effect, I spray leaves with leaf shine and wipe off excess spray with a paper towel to avoid burning them. Care for exotic leaves as you would cut flowers.

My favorites:
- The shiny philodendron, as large as 30 inches by 15 inches, allows me to wrap long stems or vases and make bold visual statements. You can also split the leaf with a knife lengthwise for a more economical usage.
- The wide aspidistra leaf, 24 inches by 4 inches, allows me to wrap the stems of a hand-tied bouquet or to make a giant ribbon at the neck of a vase.
- With the shiny burgundy red ti leaf, 12 inches by 3 inches, I can line the inside of a vase or wrap the stems of a small hand-tied bouquet.

Grasses

Most of my arrangements contain grass strands. Variegated lily grass comes in green or white, has soft edges, and can be 20 inches long by ¼ inch in size. You must take precautions on the other hand when handling the sharp-edged bear grass, a dark green 40 inches by ¼ inch. I choose one or the other, depending on the length needed, to wrap the outside of a vase, make a ribbon, or cover raffia.

Dried and Preserved Elements

From dried and colored wheat to giant bamboo poles, to coconut husks or painted dried vines, there are numerous items to choose from. I particularly favor an arrangement featuring one ingredient only (see pages 24 and 28, Huon vines and wheat; page 15, Howard bamboo) but will also mix them with fresh flowers. On page 202 (Olivier) you can see a fall cornucopia where dried mushrooms and fresh dahlias coexist. Or see pages 120 and 121 (Carroll), a console decorated with a variety of fresh and preserved topiaries.

For dried arrangements made with floral foam, make sure not to soak it beforehand! These organic sculptures will last for many years. Remove dust with a blow dryer and recycle them into new compositions.

Artificial Flowers and Plants

I am thrilled by the progress made in this industry. Today, silk flowers, artificial succulents, and delicate leaves are almost impossible to distinguish from the real thing. Budget-minded flower lovers have their pick without the seasonal constraints.

As I am lucky enough to have access to fresh flowers year round, I take advantage of the artificial flower trade to search for fantastic elements such as the silver-painted phalaenopsis, which I staged with real ones (see page 198, Olivier, media room). On page 111 right (Guiliano, living room), you will see a giant artificial agave I decided to tie in a knot for an elegant but whimsical look.

Stone

I mainly choose natural-looking black or beige ornamental stones, 1½ inches in size, to landscape my orchid gardens. For plants, I line the bottom of a container with cheaper stones to drain excess water. Small red and green stones, sold for aquariums, decorate my cactus gardens.

Floral Foam

This generally dark green, dense, spongelike material is used to hold cut flowers and branches in place, as well as to hydrate them. It is the secret tool of many sumptuous arrangements. In most cases, you will be working with the brick-shaped floral foam (9 inches by 4 inches by 3 inches). Always soak the floral foam at least 30 minutes before use (unless you are using dried or preserved elements). Remember to protect your work area from water stains, as the soaked brick will seep a little water. Once soaked, the brick is very easy to cut and to shape with a knife; it feels like cutting through butter. You can shape bricks to fit inside square and rectangular vases and even round bowls. Do not worry about having to make the floral foam sphere shown on page 222 for the Romantic White Rose Orb. You can purchase it ready-made, and spheres even come in different sizes.

Cut the end of the stems of the elements you will stick in the floral foam at an angle, about 2 inches long, for smoother penetration and best hydration. Always place your element vertically into the foam, level to its neighbors. At the end, make sure all the floral foam is hidden.

Add water mixed with floral food every other day to moisten the floral foam of a finished arrangement. You can easily remove wilted flowers or leaves without destroying your composition and replace them with fresh ones, for a longer-lasting arrangement.

With dried or artificial elements, which of course do not need hydration, you will work with dry floral foam. Floral foam can be purchased in craft or floral supply stores and on the Internet. I prefer the Oasis brand. Check out their website at www.oasisfloral.com.

BASIC TOOLS

The items on this list should be accessible to you when making any type of fresh bouquet. You can purchase the following tools at your local hardware or floral supply store, as well as on the Internet.

- Knife to cut flower stems at an angle. I use a Swiss Army pocketknife, but any sharp paring knife will do.
- Pruning shears to cut branches and bind wire
- Scissors
- Tape measure
- Watering can

- Sprayer
- Flower food. Always mix into water before filling the vase. I prefer the Floralife brand in liquid form.

OTHER FLORAL SUPPLIES

This list includes every item needed to make the recipes in this book. Most of my arrangements require waterproof green tape and wire-bound raffia. You can purchase the following tools at your local craft and floral supply store, as well as on the Internet.

- Floral foam bricks (9 inches by 4 inches by 3 inches) and spheres
- Raffia in natural color or green; choose green when working with stems and leaves, the natural color with brown elements
- Natural color wire-bound raffia
- Half-inch waterproof green tape
- Bamboo sticks ¼ inch in diameter to support orchid stems or to build a bamboo gate
- Leaf shine spray to polish the leaves. Use sparingly and wipe the sprayed leaf with a paper towel to remove excess product and avoid burns. I prefer the Pokon brand.
- Water gel crystals to give a gelled effect to the water in a clear vase. Let solidify overnight.
- Florist flower color powder to dye fresh water or gelled water
- Floral adhesive glue
- Cork coasters trimmed to fit exactly under the base of your vases to protect your furniture

BASIC CONTAINERS

You probably already have many vases in various sizes and different styles, which you rarely use, tucked away in cupboards. Now is the time to rediscover them. Take them out of hiding and place them on a table. Study each one to figure out what type of arrangement it can hold. Assess how many stems will fit into its neck. Will it best showcase short or long stems? Which one will proudly display tall branches?

Once you have even a vague picture in your mind of the general size and shape of the arrangement your containers will hold, start walking around your home and try placing each empty container on different surfaces, obvious and not so obvious—such as right on the floor or in the hearth (see page 105, Anderson, fireplace). Tall creations can soften a corner (see the pampas grass on page 46, Kennedy, dining area) and short ones can make a statement in a bookshelf (see page 193, Olivier, bookshelf). Seek out vases in your collection that would group well together. A stylish cluster of arrangements will achieve a stunning impact.

Clear vases allow you to play with the consistency and color of the water. Opaque ones will conveniently hide stems and construction materials. I have listed basic sizes and shapes to work with. Choose the style of the container that best fits your space.

- A round or square 5-inch vase for hand-tied bouquets
- A cylinder vase 12 to 14 inches high for tall flowers
- A bud vase for a single flower head
- A long rectangular vase 10 inches long by 4 inches high by 4 inches deep for centerpieces
- A bowl 8 inches in diameter and 4 inches deep for single-stem plants
- A dish 8 inches in diameter and 4 inches deep for a centerpiece
- To protect your furniture, place a thin cork coaster under every container and make sure it doesn't show.

SUPPLIERS

The magnificence of your bouquet depends heavily on the quality of its individual elements. In New York City we are fortunate to have wonderful suppliers, most of them still located in the flower district on 28th Street between 6th and 7th Avenues. Regrettably the flower district is shrinking, as soaring real-estate prices drive away the small family-owned businesses that have catered to flower lovers for decades.

In this magical market, business starts as early as 5 AM and the activity will slow by 11 AM. Several times a week I get up at dawn and visit my suppliers. Always open to new discoveries, I purchase precious flowering beauties for my clients, stores, and special events. The atmosphere is intoxicating. The ballet of thousands of flowers, plants, and trees being unloaded from the backs of trucks onto the sidewalks and hastily ushered into the stores; the explosion of colors and shapes once you enter the shop; hints of scent emanating from fragrant blooms on the shelves; the desire to touch, cradle, and connect with each specimen; the flower lingo exchanged with colleagues—these are the reasons I will always seek out flower markets not only in New York, but wherever I travel.

I highly recommend that you take an early-morning stroll down this bustling city street and discover shops crammed with the most diverse and precious varieties of cut flowers, orchid plants, flowering branches, and exotic leaves. Shops offering fabulous dried elements as well as hand-crafted artificial flowers are also conveniently located along 28th Street. Although a good number of them are wholesalers, you will never leave empty-handed. I have listed for you both wholesale and retail shops, as wholesalers often have very informative websites and will give specific care instructions for the varieties they carry. Of course, I encourage you to discover your own local flower market and develop relationships with the knowledgeable vendors in your area.

- *Jamali Garden Supplies* at 149 West 28th Street. Phone: (212) 244-4373. Website: http://www.jamaligarden.com. You will find here the listed floral tools, containers, stones, and also whimsical holiday decorative elements.
- *Planter Resource Inc.* at 150 West 28th Street. Phone: (212) 206-7687. Website: http://www.planterresource.com. Specializes in planters and vases of all sizes and shapes.
- *Caribbean Cuts* at 120 West 28th Street. Phone: (212) 924-6969. Website: http://www.caribbeancuts.com. This store sells imported tropical flowers and foliage from around the world.
- *Major Wholesale Florists, Inc.* at 41 West 28th Street (phone: 212-686-0368; website: http://www.majorwholesaleflorist.com) and *US Evergreens Inc.* at 805 Avenue of the Americas (phone: 212-741-5300) for flowering branches.
- *G. Page Wholesale Flowers* at 120 West 28th Street. Phone: (212) 741-8928. Website: http://www.gpage.com. A strictly wholesale seller of fresh local and imported cut flowers. Check out their website for seasonal listings.
- *PNK Silk Flowers Corporation* at 117 West 28th Street (phone: 212-736-8156) and *Center of Floral Design* at 145 West 28th Street (phone: 212-279-5044) offer artificial flowers, plants, and trees.
- *Dry Nature Designs Inc.* at 245 West 29th Street. Phone: (212) 695-4104. Website: http://www.drynature.com. Dry branches, tree trunks, and flowers.

ACKNOWLEDGMENTS

From the start, my dear friend Micky Palmer Boulud, with her flair and positive energy, was the inspiration for this book. Throughout the years, she has shared my ideas, my passions, my *folies*, and my doubts. Her sweet guidance and focus helped make this book into a reality.

The warm welcome of my friends and clients showcased here allowed me to create the perfect landscapes for my arrangements. I thank them from the bottom of my heart for opening their homes so graciously, and for their infinite patience with our truckloads of flowers, leaves, branches, and plants. I am forever grateful.

Our photographer, Phillip Ennis, captured my vision to perfection and beautifully depicted nature's intimate soul. His art shines throughout the pages. We worked together very closely and exchanged many wonderful artistic ideas.

Writer Sylvie Bigar beautifully captured the emotions I wished to share with my readers, as well as my personality. Our voices were always in tune, and it was a joy to convey our common passion for flowers through her fine prose.

Peter Borland, my passionate editor, has become a true friend as he steered our project with utter professionalism and elegance. He supported my vision while encouraging creativity and freedom of expression. I envy his multifaceted talent and admire his brilliant way with words.

Publisher Judith Curr, with her artistic sensibility and impeccable eye, made herself available to discuss any of my crazy ideas. Her enthusiasm for the world of floral artistry touched me deeply.

The wonderful team at Atria Books worked diligently to create my first book, and I thank them all profusely for their dedication. Special thanks to Isolde Sauer, Anthony Newfield, Nick Simonds, Dana Sloan, Jim Thiel, and also to Anne Cherry, Richard Defendorf, Elinor Schwartz Hnizdo, Kyle Kabel, Jacqueline Lee, Amy Ryan, James Walsh, Nancy Wolff, and Toby Yuen.

Art director Julian Peploe is responsible for the gorgeous layout. His talent in telling my story enhances the beauty of the photography.

Drew Kelly photographed the recipes with skill and talent. Thanks to his brilliant eye, I know his path will shine.

Janis Donnaud, my wonderful literary agent, believed in this project from the get-go and was instrumental in its development.

A special thank-you to the kind and brilliant Lili Lynton, who is always there for me.

Carine Bonnet, Lilyann Schlemon, Danielle Venokur, and Veramah Hall daily help me extend the boundaries of my profession. Pauline Benroubi, my wonderful and trusted assistant, keeps me grounded and skillfully coordinates the many facets of my work.

My fabulous design team—Santiago Neri, Dario Garcia, Rigo Gaspar, Fumie Mori, Lisa Oberholzer-Gee, Scott Robertson, and Emmanuel Delangle—always amazes me with their creativity. Alexandra Bartholomew and Emily Donofrio represent L'Olivier Floral Atelier with style and skill. June Leibowitz, Monica Wunderlich, Beth Twersky, as well as Lucino, Miguel, Marisol, Juan, Augustin, Raymundo Huerta, Bernardo Bravo, Florentino, and Rodolfo Vidals, make all things possible.

I also would like to thank and mention Monty Zullo (who helped me become a New Yorker), Monique Boutoille, Dale Black, Nancy Rodgers, Sarah Scango, Sibel Memelstein, Nicolas Cogrel, Louis Gagliano, Stefan Handl, Virginie Zaroff, Cristofer Mooney, Holly Stingley, Andria Kyriakides, Nova Rizzo, Jimmy Cellam, Marcel Lecoufle, and Penja Feuillage.

My bouquets and arrangements would not exist without the fine work of my trusted suppliers: G. Page Wholesale Flowers; Major Wholesale Florist; Harvest Wholesale Floral; Hilverda De Boer; Flower Council of Holland; Caribbean Cuts; Dutch Flower Line; Associated Cut Flower; J & P Flowers; Fisher & Page; Holiday Flower & Plant; US Evergreens; Foliage Garden; Ruth Fischl; and Party Rental.

Finally, I would not have been able to pursue this dream without my loyal clients' support and encouragement. I welcome their creative input and thoroughly enjoy our exchanges. I feel grateful to be included in their lives through their family celebrations and gatherings.

Et à toute ma famille: depuis notre Provence natale, vous m'avez toujours encouragé et vous avez toujours cru en moi. Merci.

Phillip Ennis:

Every so often I am invited to be a part of a special project. This book is one such project. I see beautiful places all the time. Olivier brings a new level of beauty, style, and elegance wherever we shoot. Thank you to Olivier for teaching me much more about arranging flowers than I could ever have imagined and for trusting my aesthetic to work with his to create "our" work. Thank you to everyone on Olivier's staff, especially Pauline, for keeping the flowers coming and the schedule on track. Peter, thanks for keeping us all together throughout the project. Thank you, Micky, for pushing us forward to keep the pace. Your charm was of course always anticipated, but it was the Payard sandwiches and éclairs that really got us going! For that a most special thanks! And also thank you to Sylvie for making my pictures sound so good!

And finally I would like to acknowledge the usual unsung heroes who make these photographs spectacular, my assistants—Glenn Callahan, Bill Combes, and Alex Jaffer—who schlep equipment up and down stairs, across fields and city streets, and set up my cameras and lights, many times on instinct, and never tell me "that's enough" when I want to do just one more shot. And last, but certainly not least, thanks to Rob Reilly for your talents in making my photos really sing.

Sylvie Bigar:

Un grand merci to Micky Palmer Boulud and Olivier Giugni for welcoming me onto your team. Thank you Peter Borland at Atria Books for your constant support; and to Janis Donnaud, who tied all the loose ends together. Phillip Ennis's glorious photographs helped bridge Olivier's stunning ephemeral creations into artistry. And *merci aussi* to my incredible husband, Stephen, who constantly shows me that passionate hard work is the key to happiness.

ART CREDITS

The author and publisher would like to thank the following sources for their kind permission to reproduce the works of art that appear in the homes featured in this book. Every effort has been made to contact the copyright holders, but we would be happy to correct any errors or omissions in future editions.

Pages ii and 77: Joel Grey, *Throne*, 2007, C-print

Pages ii and 77: Robert Rauschenberg, *Pages and Fuses,* 1974

Pages ii and 77: Richard Tuttle, *Lake,* 1968, dyed cloth

Pages vi and 80: George Talbot Kelly, *Village near Kaf Zeyat Egypt,* 1861

Page 9: Lin Dan, Monochromatic sun flower prints

Page 23: artist unknown, color photograph of a water lily farm and young woman

Page 28: William Morris Machado, *Untitled 96,* Acrylic on canvas

Page 41: Kara Walker, *Testimony,* 2005, two works from a group of five, Photogravure, Sheet size: 22.5 x 31 inches (57.2 x 78.7 cm) each

Page 42: David Rankin, *Crossings,* 2006, Painting on canvas

Page 51: Andy Spence, *Untitled (wraparound #2),* 2007, paper on wood panel, 12 x 12 x 3 in., frontview

Pages 83 and 84: Albert Watson, *Abas Chalai,* Marrakech, Morocco, 1997

Page 92: Pál Fried, title unknown

Page 98: Man Ray, "Noire et Blanche, 1926," © 2010 Man Ray Trust/Artists Rights Society (ARS), NY/ADAGP, Paris

Page 109: Man Ray, "Kiki's Lips," © 2010 Man Ray Trust/Artists Rights Society (ARS), NY/ADAGP, Paris

Pages 117 and 119: Andy Warhol, *Marilyn,* © 2010 The Andy Warhol Foundation for the Visual Arts, Inc./Artists Rights Society (ARS), New York

Pages 120, 121, and 122: Alexander Vethers, *Into the Per-fection of the Moment,* Place de la Concorde, 1989, black and white C-print

Page 145: Manolo Valdés, *Perfil con Mantilla,* 2008, Collage

Page 146: Billy Sullivan, "Agyness & Josh," 2008, Digital C-print, framed, 16.25 x 24.25 inches, Edition 1/1 (unique print)

Pages 146 and 147: Nan Goldin, "Joey Dressed for Wigstock, NYC," 1991

Page 146: McDermott and McGough, title unknown

Page 151: Michael Vollbracht, *J.F.K. Jr.,* 1996, Mixed media

Page 156: Robert Motherwell, Untitled from The Basque Suite, 1970–1971, Silkscreen on paper; edition of 150, 41 × 28¼ in. (104.1 x 71.7 cm.), Private Collection, Art © Dedalus Foundation, Inc./Licensed by VAGA, New York, NY

Page 158: Michael Vollbracht, *Portrait of Olivier,* 2007, Oil on canvas

Page 161: Horst P. Horst, "Estrella Boissevain Fashion with Easel" 1938 © Horst P. Horst/Art + Commerce

Page 161: Michael Vollbracht, *Upside Down Matisse,* 2009, Oil on canvas

Page 172: Ilse BING (1899–1998), *Gloves* (For Harper's Bazaar), Paris, 1933, Vintage gelatin silver print

Page 173: Ilse BING (1899–1998), *Gold Lame Slippers,* 1935, Vintage gelatin silver print, © Estate of Ilse Bing

Pages 181 and 187: Donald Baechler, *Memory & Illusion (Globe),* 1998, Acrylic and fabric collage on canvas, 111×122 in.

Pages 184 and 185: Tom Shannon, *Serene in Suspense,* 1999, Aqua resin, magnet, aluminum

Page 198: Erik Sampers, *Breath of Life*

Pages 200, 201, and 202: Alexander Vethers, *Into the Perfection of the Moment,* Parc des Tuileries, 1989, black and white C-print

INDEX

253